HENRY LITCHFIELD WEST

FEDERAL POWER

ITS GROWTH AND NECESSITY

Elibron Classics
www.elibron.com

Elibron Classics series.

ISBN 1-4021-4141-6 (paperback)
ISBN 1-4212-7531-7 (hardcover)

This Elibron Classics Replica Edition is an unabridged facsimile of the edition published by George H. Doran Company, New York.

FEDERAL POWER: ITS GROWTH AND NECESSITY

HENRY LITCHFIELD WEST

FEDERAL POWER:

ITS GROWTH *and* NECESSITY

BY

HENRY LITCHFIELD WEST

FORMER COMMISSIONER OF THE DISTRICT OF COLUMBIA

NEW YORK

GEORGE H. DORAN COMPANY

PRINTED IN THE UNITED STATES OF AMERICA

TO

MARY HOPE WEST

Preface

An epoch in our national history occurred on April 6, 1917, when the people of the United States, through their representatives in Congress, declared the existence of a state of war with Germany. Since that eventful date we have witnessed a most remarkable and unprecedented exercise of Federal power. We have, without protest and even with satisfaction, accorded to the government a control over corporate and individual existence which infinitely transcends the wildest dreams of those who advocate centralized authority.

This being the case, it is worth while to review, briefly and concisely, the history of the growth of Federal power. There is a prevalent idea that the acceptance of Federal control is a matter of recent development. Nothing could be further from the truth. The belief in the necessity of nationalization had its beginning nearly three centuries ago and its persistent progress can be clearly traced through all the succeeding years.

Its course is as well-defined as that of the trickling mountain stream which deepens and widens until it is a resistless force sweeping onward to the sea. In other words, the Federal power now witnessed in unparalleled extent is the evolution of a principle to which we have grown accustomed and which we now recognize as essential to our national welfare. If we seem to be advancing with rapid and overwhelming strides, it is because the momentum has been gathering for many years. Long before the war with Germany was declared, the doctrine of States' rights had vanished and the doctrine of paramount necessity had taken its place.

Because of the vital truth underlying this doctrine, the growth of Federal power will be unchecked. Its continued manifestation upon a constantly enlarging scale is as inevitable as fate. It is easier, however, to review and analyze the past than to predict the future. We know that the character of our government, as designed by its founders, is already rapidly changing and that we are less prone than heretofore to regard our Constitution as a sacred and inviolable instrument. There is a possibility, with the integrity of the State as an essential unit disappearing, that we may be brought face to face with a one-man, bureaucratic autocracy. There is still further danger of drifting into Socialism, which cannot develop in a republic composed of independent sovereignties, but which will thrive exceedingly under the ægis of a strong centralized government. The power to determine the destiny of the nation rests with the people. It is for them to solve the problem of reconciling a democratic system of government with the exercise of Federal power. The fact that they have in the past proven their capacity for self-government is the basis for the hope that they will wisely and safely cope with the grave situation which already confronts them.

H. L. W.

Contents

FEDERAL POWER: ITS GROWTH AND NECESSITY

FEDERAL POWER: ITS GROWTH AND NECESSITY

Chapter I

THE BEGINNINGS OF FEDERALISM

MANY were the causes which led our forefathers to sail westward toward the American shores. Some came with the love of adventure, others in the hope of securing wealth. The largest proportion was dominated, unquestionably, by the desire to escape the petty annoyances of trammeled existence under tyrannical rule. They sought freedom and liberty of action. The conditions under which they lived, while not altogether unbearable, restricted private endeavor. The yoke of surveillance galled their necks, and for the privilege of governing themselves they willingly endured privation in a wilderness. To-day the American people accept without protest under a centralized government a regulation of their private conduct which makes the conditions which induced the first immigration to this country seem trivial by comparison.

Small and isolated communities may be governed with the least possible effort because they present a minimum of problems. Thus during the second half of the seventeenth century, when Massachusetts Bay was far removed in point of time from Jamestown, each American settlement governed itself, or was governed, with little difficulty. Maryland, Virginia, North Carolina and even Pennsylvania accepted a governor appointed by the English king, while in rugged New England a democratic form of government had been instituted. Peacefully and separately each colony might have pursued its way had not the increase of population and the dangers from without compelled union. In this junction of interests, made necessary by the very force of circumstances, we find the beginnings of Federalism. The people realized fully 250 years ago that there was a strength in the mass which the unit did not possess. To-day they invest the Federal government with extraordinary powers because they know that it is a far more effective agency in the accomplishment of results than any individual State can possibly be. This realization has not been suddenly acquired. It comes as the culmination of nearly three centuries of experience. Perhaps just now it is expressed more emphatically than ever before in our history but the seed was planted long ago. And because ideas which persist through long periods take firm possession of the human mind and are then difficult to eradicate, the Federalistic sentiment so prevalent to-day warrants the most serious consideration.

Three problems confronted the early colonists. The first and most important was the necessity of mutual protection against their common enemies, the Indians, Dutch and French. The second was the relation which the citizens of one colony should bear to the other. The third was the disposition to be made of fugitives from justice who fled beyond the border line of the territory in which their offense was committed. It was these factors which led to the confederation of the New England colonists in 1643. There was no hint, however, of any real union in this agreement of mutual help. On the contrary, the terms of the articles of confederation expressly reserved to each colony its own local rights and jurisdiction. They did agree, it is true, not to make war without permission of their co-partners unless suddenly invaded and also that no two colonies should join in one jurisdiction without the consent of the others, but beyond this each colony was a law unto itself. The very fact that they came together, however, with a definite idea underlying their joint action, is important. It is the fact itself, rather than the manner or the method, which is significant.

This union in 1643 between Massachusetts, New Plymouth, Connecticut and New Haven was described as a league of friendship, the identical phrase used by the thirteen colonies in 1781 when they adopted the Articles of Confederation which were the precursor of the Constitution. The details of the union were very simple. Each colony was to name two Commissioners, and if six of the eight agreed upon any question, their decision was to stand; otherwise, it was to be referred back to the colonial assemblies, in which case the agreement of all four was to be required. Provision was made in the agreement for the return of runaway slaves and fugitives from justice, but the vital principle incorporated was the recognition of intercitizenship, the inhabitants of each colony being accorded equal rights in the other colonies. It seems very absurd nowadays to read of a solemn compact which assured an equality of citizenship, but at that time it was an absolute necessity. In the early history of the Pennsylvania colony the people were highly indignant because a Delaware sheriff crossed their border in pursuit of a thief and the feeling between Massachusetts and Rhode Island was so bitter that it was dangerous for the citizen of one colony to be found within the confines of the other.

Although this particular agreement became obsolete within forty-five years and accomplished little or nothing, the germ of Federalism had been planted. As the years advanced, the people of the colonies became more and more impressed with the desirability as well as the necessity of coöperation and consolidation. In 1690 the New England colonies, together with New York, Virginia, and Maryland, made an effort to combine and, although the attempt was not successful, it gave evidence of the existence of a sentiment for union. The capture of the French fortress Louisburg, on the coast of Cape Breton, by a New England force under General Pepperell in 1745, was signalized by the "hoisting of a Union flag." William Penn, shrewd and farsighted, should, perhaps, be designated as the father of Federalism, because his plan of combination as drawn up in 1696 was a very distinct advance in the way of definite suggestion. It was unique in that, for the first time, all the colonies were included, and because it provided that the assembly of the delegates should be called "the Congress," to be presided over by a Commissioner appointed by the King. More than this, however, was the provision for the regulation of commerce between the colonies. This was the crux then, as it is now, of the Federalistic movement. It had been easy to give citizens equal consideration everywhere and to combine in self-protection against a common enemy, but experience was to prove that agreements which failed to take into consideration the very practical and material regulation of commerce by a central organization would be neither effective nor lasting. Penn's plan, although widely discussed, was not adopted, but its vital principle of union, instead of dying out, became more and more alive. Robert Livingstone in 1701 suggested combining the colonies into three distinct governments, while twenty years later the Earl of Stair proposed a union of all the American colonies and the West Indies, with local self-government guaranteed to each. Many other thinkers came forward with similar schemes of consolidation, all of them expressing more and more the spirit of ultimate concentration of a Federalistic power. Finally, in 1754, in the Albany Congress, Benjamin Franklin evolved a plan which was a tremendous stride forward. It went too far, as a matter of fact, and was rejected; but its details are worthy of consideration as showing, even at that remote day, a realization of the eventual necessity of a centralized government.

Franklin proposed a grand council of the colonies with members proportioned roughly to population, presided over by a President-General, who was to be invested with power to execute the acts of the council. This idea of an authoritative head over all the colonies was not as startling, however, as the provision that the grand council should "lay and levy general duties, imposts and taxes" proportionately upon each colony. The thought embodied in this proposition was revolutionary. It confronted the colonies with a power superior to themselves. They were to govern themselves independently, of course, but they were also to be subject to paying assessments—nobody knew how much or how little—which might be laid upon them. The assembly to which this plan was submitted, although it unanimously agreed that union was absolutely necessary for preservation, would not agree to being taxed by a central body, even though in that body the colonies were fully represented. But the inevitable was merely postponed. Less than half a century later they were to agree to a Constitution into which, through the agency of taxation and the regulation of commerce, the supremacy of Federal power was to be breathed and the nation made a living soul.

The first necessity for cohesion had been protection against the Indians. In the last quarter of the eighteenth century another danger threatened. The English government, with fatuous persistency, had not only laid undue burdens upon the colonies but had done so in a manner calculated to arouse bitter resentment. The Stamp Act, which made the colonists contribute to the revenues of the British crown although without representation in the British Parliament, was especially odious. The closing of the port of Boston and other restrictions upon navigation bore heavily upon the population, while the fact that citizens of the colonies had been denied trial by jury and had even been transported to England for trial was repugnant to every sense of justice and fair play. It became essential, if these impositions were to be removed and the colonies left in the enjoyment of their peace and liberty, that there should be concerted action. In other words, the day of individual existence was passed and the colonies were to be transformed, as some one expressed it, into a bundle of sticks which could neither be bent nor broken. The bundle was, however, rather insecurely bound. The twine—for the material did not reach the stoutness nor dignity of rope—was the Continental Congress, a body of delegates with no authority behind them except public sentiment and who conducted a war against Great Britain in a hap-hazard arrangement with the colonies. It was while this war was in progress that the Articles of Confederation were adopted. Thcy declared that the States severally entered into "a firm league of friendship with each other for their common defense, the security of their liberties, and their mutual and general welfare, binding themselves to assist each other against all force offered to, or attacks made upon, them, or any of them, on account of religion, sovereignty, trade, or any other pretense whatever." The States were not allowed to send or receive foreign embassies nor to make treaties with each other, but they could maintain war vessels "in such number as might be deemed necessary by the United States in Congress assembled, for defense of such State or its trade," while the land force could be large enough to garrison all the forts within the State These Articles of Confederation are not so important for what they contain, however, as for what they omit. The former colonies, still tenacious of their individual rights, even though willing to be associated together under the title of "The United States of America," would not yield to Congress the right to make them pay taxes. Such powers as the Continental Congress possessed without written authority were not much increased by the document creating "the league of friendship." The Congress could modestly suggest what sum might be needed to maintain the central government but it had neither power nor machinery to enforce payment. The respect, not to say reverence, shown to the State as an entity was very marked. Congress itself declared that it could not negotiate a treaty of commerce which interfered with the legislative power of the State "in imposing such imposts and duties on foreigners as their own people are subjected to." The prerogatives of the State were still further jealously guarded by a provision which gave one vote to each State and compelled the assent of nine out of the thirteen States to practically every measure which might be imposed.

Weak and disorderly, inefficient and unsatisfactory, was the government under the Articles of Confederation, and simply because the people in the new States could not appreciate fully the necessity of surrendering sovereignty and putting force behind laws. It seems ridiculous to-day that New York should have possessed the authority to pass laws—and actually did enact laws—to keep out firewood from Connecticut and garden truck from New Jersey. No wonder that the bundle of sticks began to fall apart. Separation seemed imminent. Congress, declining daily in public esteem because of its confessed impotence, was too weak to exercise any authority, and was equally helpless in the matter of raising revenues to meet current expenses. Then came the trouble with Spain over the navigation of the lower Mississippi River, which interfered with the effort to secure a commercial treaty with that country, and for the settlement of which no authority seemed to exist anywhere. Meanwhile, the rag money issued by the States was practically worthless and the lack of a secure currency occasioned great distress. Different States enacted different tariff and tonnage acts; State jealousies were easily aroused and frequently expressed. Massachusetts, for instance, although disturbed by serious internal troubles, declared that it was beneath its dignity to allow Congressional troops to set foot upon its soil. There was no such thing as national credit, while national authority was absolutely non-existent.

Under these circumstances, it was more and more borne in upon the American people that their system of self-government was vitally wrong. The very conditions under which they lived convinced them that they had not solved the problem. Fortunately there were men like George Washington to courageously point out the defect and suggest the remedy. These men appealed to what might be called the Federal spirit in the people—the spirit which, manifested in various forms during the preceding century and a half, was now to be stimulated into accomplishment. Washington insisted that there should be a central government which, in addition to possessing the power to make war and peace and conclude treaties, should also have authority to levy taxes and regulate commerce, and should completely control the executive and judicial departments. He felt, as he expressed it later, that it was impracticable to secure all the rights of independent sovereignty to each State and yet provide for the interest and safety of all. Pelatiah Webster, stating the idea more definitely, proposed "a new system of government which should act not on the States but directly upon individuals and vest in Congress full power to carry its laws into effect." The fullness of time had come; but even so, it was necessary for the men who foresaw that only in united and not divided power could the union survive, to move with caution. The famous convention of 1787, which framed the Constitution, was the outgrowth of a conference called to consider the relations between Maryland and Virginia growing out of the extension of navigation in the upper Potomac. Merely as a secondary consideration for the gathering at Annapolis was it suggested that the delegates should take up the task of amending the Articles of Confederation. The path to Federalism, while proving less arduous, was not unopposed. There were still some people who argued that the principle involved in the protest against the Stamp Act, viz., that no authority to levy taxes existed outside of the State itself, was now proposed to be violated by the creation of a central government which would exercise this power. They asked why they had fought the war of the Revolution if the independence which they had gained was thus to be ruthlessly sacrificed. This discontent found expression in the insurrection in Western Massachusetts in 1786-87, known as Shays's rebellion. Happily, however, these voices were in the minority. The great mass of people, as John Fiske so plainly shows, were more afraid of anarchy than of centralization; and anarchy was staring them in the face.

It seems strange nowadays, when we are so thoroughly accustomed to appeals for the larger exercise of Federal power, to read how the people of little over a century ago stood with anxious faces under the shadow of an impending Federal government. They accepted it with trepidation because it seemed to be their only salvation, and because there had been visible demonstration of its efficiency during the preceding one hundred and fifty years. They had learned by experience the value of united action against enemies from without, the Indians and the English. They had an idea that what had proven efficacious yesterday might be equally so to-day. What they did not foresee was that a century later the people would unite to make the strong arm of the government still stronger so as to fight enemies from within —corporate domination and the monopoly of trusts—as well as to insure the largest degree of benefit to each individual citizen of the United States.

Chapter II

THE FIRST TRIUMPH OF FEDERALISM

THE fate of the union now hung in the balance. If the States would agree to abandon their idea of independent sovereignty in order that centralized government might be established there was hope for future solidity and progress.

In selecting George Washington as the president of the Constitutional Convention the friends of Federalism gained a decided victory. It is true that as the presiding officer Washington could not participate in the debates, but he was a Federalist at heart and his influence was strong with delegates of wavering opinions. The theory of the sovereign character of the States was still uppermost in many minds and it was no easy matter for the Federalists to convince these doubters that the Federal government must possess the power to levy taxes and regulate commerce. These were the crucial points at issue. Questions as to how the representatives of the people were to be chosen; how the President should be elected and the length of his term; and whether the Federal judiciary should be elected or appointed, were mere details. The future of the government was settled when a dozen words had been written into the Constitution—"general welfare," "lay and collect taxes," and "regulate commerce among the several States." When, in addition, it was declared that all laws of the United States made in pursuance of the Constitution "shall be the supreme law of the land, and the judges in every State shall be bound thereby, anything in the constitution or laws of any States to the contrary notwithstanding," the growth of Federalism was as inevitable as fate. The seed was planted and the day of full fruition was merely a question of time. The tenth amendment to the Constitution, which prescribes that "the powers not delegated to the United States by the Constitution, nor prohibited by it to the States, are reserved to the States respectively, or to the people," was merely a sop to Cerberus. It eased the minds of the opponents of a centralized government and to that extent accomplished the purpose for which it was intended.

The victory for Federalism in the Constitution

came as the outcome of a skillfully managed contest. The States, unaware of the tremendous issues to come before the convention, sent their delegates with perfunctory credentials. New Hampshire stood practically alone in its declaration that it would not circumscribe its views "to the narrow and selfish objects of the partial convenience," and in its avowal of readiness to make every concession for the safety and happiness of the whole. When Edmund Randolph, delegate from Virginia, introduced a series of resolutions as a basis for action, he carefully avoided all reference to the levying of taxes or the regulation of commerce, although he was willing that Congress should "legislate in all cases to which the separate States are incompetent or in which the harmony of the United States may be interrupted by the exercise of individual legislation." Charles Pinckney, of South Carolina, went further and boldly proposed that Congress "shall have the power to lay and collect taxes, duties, imposts and excises." While this vital principle was being gradually impressed upon the minds of the delegates the debate proceeded. The tender sensibilities of those who still manifested some regard for the rights of the States were rudely shocked by the unqualified expressions of Alexander Hamilton. "I am convinced," he said, "that no amendment of the Confederation can answer the purpose of a good government so long as the State sovereignties in any way exist." He declared further that State distinctions and State operations must be annihilated, "and unless we do this," he added, "no good purpose can be secured." One of his reasons for electing Representatives by the people was a belief that there might come a time when State legislatures would cease and he thought that "such an event ought not to embarrass the national government." It must not be understood, however, that these radical views were uttered without arousing protest. On the contrary, Robert Yates and John Lansing, jr., delegates from New York, withdrew from the convention when they found the Federal spirit so strongly expressed and saw it being embodied in the Constitution. They hastened home to pour out their grievances into the sympathetic ear of Governor Clinton and then gave publicity to their fears. They asserted that the principles incorporated into the Constitution were destructive to civil liberty, argued that the United States could never govern the wide expanse of territory included within its borders, spoke timorously of the great cost which the national legislature would entail upon the people, and strenuously objected to New York being deprived of its most essential rights of sovereignty and placed in a dependent position.

Unnecessarily alarmed were Yates and Lansing, as the future demonstrated, and yet they were not alone in their position. The Constitution was finally adopted by the convention because the country was then face to face, as it is to-day, with problems not to be solved except through the exercise of strong Federal power; but out of the sixty-five delegates designated, only thirty-nine remained in their seats to affix their signatures to the immortal document. In Virginia, Patrick Henry denounced the Constitution as a flagrant outrage upon the States and he especially criticized the opening phrase, "We, the people of the United States." He saw in these words the beginning of the end. Many Virginians shared his views—Richard Henry Lee and George Mason among the number. The final ratification by Virginia was accomplished by the narrow margin of ten votes out of a total of 165, and only because the members of the State convention had the wisdom to see that no matter how the States had been treated, the powers granted by the Constitution still remained with the people and had not in any way been abridged. As a matter of fact, time has demonstrated the accuracy of this point of view. The wide extent of power now enjoyed by the Federal government has been given to it by the people. The government has become, as some one has aptly expressed it, a creature of the masses which compose the sovereignties rather than of the sovereignties themselves.

But it was impossible in those days, with a few weak States just emerging from a long and costly war, to secure the acquiescence in Federal supremacy which is now accepted as a matter of course. "Sic transit gloria Americana," wrote Elbridge Gerry, while Samuel Chase, James Monroe, and scores of other leading men joined in the general chorus of criticism. At Albany a copy of the Constitution was publicly burned and in Rhode Island nearly 1,000 armed men, headed by a judge of the State Supreme Court, compelled the speakers at a public gathering to desist from saying anything favorable to the Constitution. To meet this hostile sentiment

Hamilton, Madison and Jay—but mainly Hamilton—wrote the Federalist papers. These cogent and logical expositions of the necessity for a Federal government are so familiar that only two observations are requisite to the purposes of this volume. The first is that they have endured. There were innumerable pamphlets in opposition to the scheme outlined in the Constitution but they have perished, save for a few rare copies now preserved in various libraries. The Federalist papers, on the other hand, have been published in many editions and still remain standard literature, a convincing illustration of the trend of the public mind. In the second place, it is worth while to note how Hamilton's predictions have been completely disproved by the experience of history. "It will always be more easy," he wrote, "for the State governments to encroach upon the national authority than for the National government to encroach upon the State authorities." This idea was several times repeated. "It should not be forgotten," he wrote again, "that a disposition in the State governments to encroach upon the rights of the Union is quite as probable as a disposition in the Union to encroach upon the rights of the State governments." A contest between the two, he declared, "will be most apt to end to the disadvantage of the Union." It is difficult to reconcile these statements with Hamilton's admittedly keen political foresight. If he did not realize that the strong central government for which he argued, a government with authority to levy taxes and regulate commerce among the States, would be more powerful than any one State, his political acumen has been over-rated; while if he did appreciate it, he deliberately misled the people in his overwhelming desire to secure the ratification of the Constitution. In either case, history has fully demonstrated the falsity of his position.

Despite much misgiving on the part of the few, the great mass of the people pushed ahead under the new Federal government, halting for a moment when they elected Jefferson to succeed Adams, but finding that Jefferson could forget his strict constructionist ideas and become an expansive nationalist when the opportunity to purchase Louisiana presented itself. Steadily the spirit of Federalism grew. There were, of course, many problems, and some outward expressions of discontent over the exercise of Federal power at the expense of the rights of the States. The conflicts were frequent and intense. In 1793, four years after the government was established, the Supreme Court of the United States, in the famous case of Chisholm *vs.* Georgia, decided that a citizen of one State could sue another State in the Federal courts. This decision laid all the States liable to suits to compel payment of debt obligations and caused much dissatisfaction and even alarm. The Georgia House of Representatives angrily declared that such assumption of Federal authority would "effectually destroy the retained sovereignty of the State," would render the States nothing but tributary corporations of the United States Government, and added that the State would not be bound by the judgment of the Federal court. More than this, the State legislature passed a law providing that any person attempting to carry out the decree of the Federal court by seizing property within the State should be hung without benefit of clergy. Other States, including Massachusetts and New Hampshire, also protested, but without immediate result. Five years elapsed before the ratification of the eleventh amendment to the Constitution, which forbids the extension of the judicial power of the United States to any suit commenced or prosecuted against one of the United States by citizens of another State. The remonstrances of one or two States against alleged degradation at the hands of the Federal government were certainly not provocative of swift redress on the part of the people.

Still more illustrative of the growth of the Federal sentiment even in those early days was the reception given to the protest of Virginia and Kentucky against the Alien and Sedition Laws. The Alien Law gave the President power to order out of the United States all aliens whom he judged dangerous to the peace and safety of the country, or who he suspected were concerned in any treasonable or secret machinations against the government: while the Sedition Law made it an offense punishable by fine and imprisonment to "write, print, utter, or publish, any false, scandalous, or malicious writings against the government, either house of Congress, or the President." Immediately the legislatures of Virginia and Kentucky passed resolutions clearly defining their opinion as to the relation of a State toward the Federal government. The original draft of the Kentucky declaration, written by Jefferson, was an admirable document, so far as its presentation of the rights of a State was concerned. "This commonwealth is determined," the resolutions asserted, "as it doubts not its co-States are, to submit to undelegated and consequently unlimited powers in no man, or body of men, on earth." There was also in the protest a distinct assertion of the right of nullification—a theory later to be critically precipitated by South Carolina. It was, in effect, a contention that the citizen owed his first allegiance to his State, a principle which also later found its exemplification at the outbreak of the Civil War. The Virginia resolutions were prepared by Madison and were naturally less belligerent in tone, but even they called upon all the States to co-operate with Virginia in necessary and proper measures for "maintaining unimpaired the authorities, rights and liberties reserved to the States respectively, or to the people." The value of the recital of this incident is not in the fact that the resolutions were passed, for that was quite understandable, but in the attitude of the other States. This shows how thoroughly the people had already become inoculated with Federalism. Although the resolutions were transmitted to all the States, there was no very general affirmative response. On the contrary, Delaware regarded them as "a very unjustifiable interference with the general government and the constituted authorities of the United States," while Massachusetts went still further and denied the authority of any State to call into question the constitutionality of a Federal law. Pennsylvania, in the same spirit, declared that such resolutions were calculated to destroy the very existence of the government, while New York, Connecticut, New Hampshire and Vermont all expressed dissent from Virginia's position.

Although the objectionable laws were eventually repealed, the people were thus beginning to acknowledge the commanding position of the Federal government and were inclining to the belief that what the government did was right. The new idea was not, however, universal. The country was still divided into two factions—one upholding the sovereign character of the States and the other insisting upon larger powers for the Federal government. The election of Thomas Jefferson to the presidency was a momentary victory for the former. The defeat of the Federal party occurred in November, 1800. Jefferson could not be inaugurated until March 4, 1801. During the four months that intervened the Federalists executed the most remarkable *coup d'état* in American history. They had lost the executive and legislative branches of the government. They determined, however, to hold the judicial. Here again we find Hamilton's judgment to be utterly at variance with facts. In his Federalist papers, discussing the judiciary, he had minimized this branch of the government. According to his view, the judiciary would never be a serious factor. He asserted that the judiciary, from the very nature of its functions, would be the least dangerous to the political rights of the Constitution. "The executive," he said, "not only dispenses the honors but holds the sword of the community. The legislature not only commands the purse, but prescribes the rules by which the duties and the rights of every citizen are to be regulated. The judiciary, on the contrary, has no influence either over the sword or the purse; no direction either of the strength or the wealth of the society; and can take no active resolution whatever. It may truly be said to have neither force nor will, but merely judgment." For these reasons he concluded that "the judiciary is beyond comparison the weakest of the three departments of power."

But now the Federalist party was to demonstrate that instead of being the weakest, the judiciary was the strongest of the three departments of power, for it enacted, on the eve of its ejection from control, a law adding six new circuit and twenty-two district judges to the Federal judiciary. More than this, President Adams, within twenty days of the expiration of his term, took John Marshall out of his cabinet, in which he was Secretary of State, and appointed him Chief Justice of the Supreme Court of the United States. The importance of this action upon the development of the Federalistic spirit in the United States cannot be overestimated. In the appointment of Marshall the doom of the doctrine of the sovereignty of the States was sealed. Still further, the time was to come, in the evolution of Federalism, when the Supreme Court would direct the strength and especially the wealth of society by decisions affecting the organization of gigantic corporations, involving the regulation and distribution of swollen fortunes.

Chapter III

THE FEDERALISTIC INFLUENCE OF JOHN MARSHALL

THE period between 1801 and 1835 marked another epoch in the growth of the Federalistic spirit in the United States. During these thirty-four years John Marshall, of Virginia, was Chief Justice of the Supreme Court of the United States. It was the formative period of the nation. The Constitution had been adopted, it is true, but the great Federal principle which underlay its adroit phrasing was but dimly realized. Men viewed its provisions according to their own convictions. There had been no definite expression and upon the character of this expression depended the future of the republic.

Marshall spoke the words which emphasized nationality. It is useless now to speculate upon what might have been our destiny if a man of the Jeffersonian manner of thinking had been placed in the position which Marshall occupied. It is possible the whole trend of our history might have been changed and that instead of a centralized government, steadily increasing in strength, we should have had a league of independent but weak States, lacking the binding force of nationality. So great was the influence which Marshall exerted, so lasting was the effect of his decisions, that some reference to his personality is not inappropriate, even though the story of his life may not be unfamiliar. In following the growth of Federal power in the United States his figure occupies such a commanding position that it can neither be overlooked nor minimized. He had been rightfully characterized as a nation-builder. In the face of a hostile executive and a hostile Congress he upheld the banner of nationalism and not only his courage and force but the far-reaching effect of his views transformed the judiciary from a coördinate into a dominating factor in our system of government. To-day we are beginning to question whether the courts have the right to the last word upon questions affecting the interpretation of constitutional provisions —a subject inviting discussion were it not for the fact that it would lead too far afield. Suffice it to say that it will take some time to dislodge from the public mind the idea of judicial supremacy inculcated by Marshall and coming down to us through many years.

Profound convictions are not uttered upon the spur of the moment but are the concrete expression of accumulated observation and associations. This was eminently true of Marshall's decisions. The judgments which he rendered as Chief Justice of the Supreme Court of the United States were as inevitable as the following of an effect upon its cause. He had no hesitation in ascribing his devotion to the idea of union, and to a government competent to its preservation, at least as much to current events as to theoretical reasoning. He was imbued, he said, with the maxim, "United we stand, divided we fall," and it became a part of his being. In the army, for he had served with great credit during the Revolution, he was confirmed in the habit of considering "America as my country and Congress as my government." The lesson of the war with Great Britain, when an almost impotent Congress had more than once jeopardized victory, had not been lost upon his observing mind. He had seen how the jealousies of the States had intervened; how the lack of Federal power in the government had paralyzed its efforts; and he felt that the republic could not survive unless all this was changed. In so far as he had been able he had upheld the hands of Washington and the Federalists. He had fought for the ratification of the Constitution in the Virginia legislature, defeating Patrick Henry by the force of logic against eloquence; he had won a seat in Congress at the hands of a hostile electorate through mere strength of character and personal popularity; he had defended President Adams upon the floor of the House against a resolution of censure for surrendering to the British government a sailor accused of murder; he had steadfastly maintained, in controversy with Jefferson, the Federal theory of government; and, finally, as Secretary of State under Adams, he had emphasized in his official correspondence the national character of the government which he represented. Above all, he was skilled in the law. He was, therefore, a person of no uncertain quality. He had been tried in the balance and not found wanting. President Adams was making no experiment when he selected John Marshall to be the expounder of the Federal doctrine in the court of last resort. Whether he fully appreciated the future consequences of his act may, indeed, be a matter of doubt; but history can never acquit him of indulging in the hope that in some measure, at least, he had checkmated the temporary triumph of the men who believed more in a confederation of petty but independent sovereignties than in the subordination of these jurisdictions to Federal power.

It so happened that an opportunity was immediately afforded to Marshall to emphasize his views. William Marbury, a citizen of the District of Columbia, sought to compel James Madison, Secretary of State, to deliver to him a commission of appointment as justice of the peace, signed by President Adams and to which the seal of the State Department had been affixed, but which had not been delivered before Mr. Adams vacated the presidential office. Chief Justice Marshall, although he did not issue the mandamus, decided that the Secretary of State ought to surrender the commission and then took occasion to enunciate his ideas as to the nature of the government. He upheld the Constitution as supreme, not to be violated by any of the coördinate branches of the Government. He declared that the Supreme Court had the right to review the acts of the national legislature and of the executive—a declaration accepted to-day without protest, but very revolutionary to the public mind in 1803. Jefferson, for instance, uttered fierce denunciation, and one of Marshall's colleagues on the bench exclaimed that "the American people can no longer enjoy the blessings of a free government whenever the State sovereignties shall be prostrated at the feet of the general government." Jefferson, foreseeing and fearing the power of the Federal judiciary, sought to embarrass its operations by instigating at least two impeachments, one of which succeeded on account of the admitted incapacity of the judge, and the other ignominiously failed.

In the midst of the storm which he had created Marshall pursued his undaunted way. Decision followed decision, each one striking more and more at the so-called sovereignty of the States and extolling not only the necessity but the benefits of a strong Federal government. In the case of the United States against Peters, he declared that the legislature of a State could not annul the judgment of the courts of the United States and destroy the rights acquired under those judgments. In the case of Fletcher against Peck he decided that the constitutionality of a law passed by a State legislature was a question within the jurisdiction of a

Federal court. In McCulloch *vs.* Maryland the decision was to the effect that a State had no right to lay a tax upon an institution chartered by Congress, the statement being made that if one Federal institution could be taxed, so could the mail, the mint and the custom-house; and with the added remark that the American people "did not desire their government to depend upon the States." The supremacy of a Congressional enactment to any State law was asserted in the case of Cohens *vs.* Virginia, which concerned a man arrested and fined under the State law for selling lottery tickets, although the lottery existed in Washington under the authority of a Federal statute. The State of Virginia was emphatically advised that the Supreme Court of the United States had jurisdiction over cases arising under Federal laws.

It is impossible, of course, even to mention, much less review in detail, the thirty-six decisions which Mr. Marshall wrote in connection with Federal questions, but there are two others to which reference must be made on account of their ultimate effect in determining the Federal character of the government. The first was the Dartmouth College case, in which the constitutional provision against the impairment of an obligation of contract was held to apply to a charter granted to a corporation notwithstanding State legislation. This decision stands to-day as the main element of stability in corporate enterprise. The other case was that of Gibbons *vs.* Ogden. The problem in this case would not be deemed to-day worthy of a moment's consideration and is only cited as showing how jealous were the States of their independence in the early stages of our history. Two citizens of New York, Fulton and Livingstone, had been granted by the legislature of that State the exclusive right to navigate the waters of the State with steamboats and had sub-leased the privilege to Ogden. A citizen of New Jersey named Gibbons, operating under a coasting trade license issued by the Federal government under a Federal law, had invaded the New York waters and had been ordered by the New York courts to desist. He thereupon appealed to the United States Supreme Court for protection in the use of a navigable river. It seems trivial enough nowadays, this controversy over New York's claim to exclusive jurisdiction, but it was no simple matter then. The contention of the State was swept aside with ruthless hand. More than this, the power of the United States to regulate commerce among the States was set forth with such lucidity and emphasis that the principles which Marshall enunciated remain practically unchanged to the present day. The authority of the Federal government in dealing with commerce, while resting primarily upon the Constitution, was given a width of range in this decision, written nearly a century ago, which still stands unrestricted. "In war," said Marshall, "we are one people. In making peace we are one people. In all commercial relations we are one and the same people." This was the keynote of his views. The distinction which he drew between the people and the States must be borne in mind to-day when it is the people who, through the Federal Congress, are gradually atrophying the legislatures of the States.

Larger and larger were the powers and authorities which, in opinion succeeding opinion, Marshall gave not only to the Supreme Court but to the President and to Congress, all of them agents of the Federal government. There were strict and narrow constructionists of the Constitution in those days—many more, in fact, than there are to-day—but Marshall brushed them aside with scant consideration. To his mind they were obstacles in the path of progress. He scorned their reasoning, under which, to use his own words, the Constitution would still be a magnificent structure to look at, but totally unfit for use. Under the tremendous force of his logic, coupled with a stern realization of its truth, the Federal instinct developed. The American people began to accept largely, if not universally, the doctrine of "the subordination of the parts to the whole, rather than the complete independence of any one of them." They were compelled to agree with him, even against their will, that the government would be "a mere shadow unless invested with large portions of that sovereignty which belongs to independent States." Perhaps, after all, they were most impressed with the depth and sincerity of his convictions. Certainly sentences like these, used in beginning one of his decisions, must have made a profound impression upon the public mind:

The Constitution of our country, in its most interesting and vital parts, is to be considered; the conflicting powers of the government of the Union and of its members, as marked in that Constitution, are to be discussed and an opinion given, which may essentially influence the great operations of the government. No tribunal can approach such a question without a deep sense of its importance, and of the awful responsibility involved in its decision. But it must be decided peacefully or remain a source of hostile legislation, perhaps of hostility of a still more serious nature; and if it is to be so decided, by this tribunal alone can the decision be made. On the Supreme Court of the United States has the Constitution of our country devolved this important duty.

In this reverential and solemn spirit did Marshall approach and, with his colleagues, decide the momentous questions that determined the absolute unity and solidity of these United States. When he wrote these words, he was not building ignorantly, even though he may have been building wiser than he knew. He had the eye of a seer and foresaw plainly that if his views remained as the law of the land there could be but one outcome, the obliteration of State lines. The period which he pictured is upon us. Surely the thirty-four years during which he sat upon the bench must be regarded as epochal. It stands out in history as a milestone from which to measure further advance.

Beginning his career upon the Supreme Bench with the executive and Congress and a majority of people anti-Federalist in their views, Marshall lived to see the river of Federalism grow wider and deeper. His first decision, in the case of Marbury *vs.* Madison, coming, as it did, like a thunderbolt out of a clear sky, had aroused indignant protest; his last decision, although no less uncompromising in its limitation on supposed rights of the States, was accepted as expressing what had become a settled principle. In the meantime much had happened. The War of 1812, for instance, had done much to awaken national spirit and the Star-Spangled Banner, as the national emblem, filled the public eye. There were propositions in Congress relating to a new national currency, a national university and the national improvement of highways. The act re-chartering the Bank of the United States was passed in 1816, the institution being destined later to figure prominently in a bitter dispute as to the abuse of its great power. In the same year a tariff law was passed and Congress also provided for national improvements. All these extensions of Federal authority were not accomplished, however, without much protest and criticism. This antagonism is mentioned merely to emphasize the fact that it was futile and has been forgotten. Over all was spread the ægis of Marshall's decisions.

These inspired the American people with the greatness of the government they had formed. Their principles have since found permanent lodgment in the American mind because they were founded upon everlasting verity.

Chapter IV

THE CIVIL WAR AND ITS CONSEQUENCES

THE period between the death of Chief Justice Marshall and the beginning of the Civil War was notable for a marked indisposition on the part of the American people squarely to meet the issue of a centralized government.

While the national spirit grew, there was still a prevalent idea that the States were worthy of consideration. Even though the national pride had been stimulated by the victories of Perry at Lake Erie and Jackson at New Orleans, there had been a gathering of New England men at Hartford to protest against the powers of Congress in matters pertaining to war and the laying of embargoes, while there was a strong objection to the refusal of the United States to pay for the expense of defending Massachusetts and Connecticut because those States would not place their militia under the control of the Federal government. Jefferson sought to check the tide of Federal power by frowning upon Congressional appropriations for local improvements and Madison vetoed a bill which carried money for the Cumberland road. Whenever the country was brought squarely up against the question as to which was supreme, the nation or the State, some way was found to avoid a direct answer. There was compromise in the admission of Missouri, the demand of the settlers of that territory that they be granted the right to hold slaves being accorded, but it being also agreed that the slave-holding area otherwise should not extend north of a line drawn west of Missouri on the parallel of 36° 30′. The rights of a territory, or even a State, under the Constitution, were still unsettled when Kansas and Nebraska sought admission, and when Congress threw the problem back to the people the struggle between the free-soilers and the would-be slave-holding element led to sanguinary encounters. In the case of South Carolina the question of State rights was acutely presented. The South Carolina legislature declared that the Federal tariff should be regarded as null and void within the State borders. This aroused the anger of the irascible Jackson, who, although he had once advised Congress against all encroachments upon the legitimate sphere of State sovereignty, now threatened to personally hang upon the nearest tree any person who disobeyed the Federal law. "The Federal union," he dramatically exclaimed, "it must be preserved." Calhoun insisted that a State had the right to nullify, while Webster argued with wonderful eloquence and logic for national supremacy. Still, no one seemed to care to meet the issue face to face and again there was a compromise in which Congress agreed to respect the basis of South Carolina's protest and adjust the tariff upon lines which were not wholly objectionable to the South.

It is not strange that in those days men were unwilling to go to the extreme of full acceptation of Federal domination. It is true that the country was developing tremendously, that new States were being added to thc union, that the railroads and the telegraph were about to become powerful factors in the growth of commerce, and that it was evident that the United States was destined to become one of the great nations of the world. At the same time, the old Federalist party had practically disappeared; there was still the memory of the part which the States had played in the formation of the union; and there was no desire to make complete the partial surrender of State jurisdiction and State operation which had made the union possible. No man, however, can serve two masters. There could not be an equality between the State and the nation. The weaker must give way to the stronger. The part could not be greater than the whole. It was inevitable that the question had to be settled, even though the decision necessitated a fratricidal struggle. Even when the clouds were darkest the regard for the rights of the States was evident. The political conventions of 1860 carefully ignored all reference to the troublous issue, and even President Lincoln, in his inaugural address, while he emphasized the perpetuity of the union, was willing to agree that the *status quo* should be preserved. Viewed through the perspective of time, the most remarkable thing about the generation between Marshall's judicial service and the Civil War was the reluctance with which the nation approached the conclusion that the Federal government is, and must necessarily be, supreme.

Then came the war, and with it an exercise of Federal power far beyond the wildest flights of the Hamiltonian imagination. There was no longer thought of compromise or possibility of evasion. The issue had to be squarely met. There was some muttering as larger and larger powers were assumed by the heroic Lincoln and by Congress, while the restrictions of the Constitution were ignored. In his inaugural message Lincoln had suggested that "the power confided to me will be used to hold, occupy and possess the property and places belonging to the Government and collect the duties and imposts, but beyond what will be necessary for these objects there will be no invasion." More than this, he had discussed in temperate fashion the maintenance inviolate of the rights of the States and had quoted with apparent approval the constitutional guarantee for the return of escaped slaves. When, after Sumter had been fired upon, Congress met on the 4th of July, he submitted an argument aimed at the destruction of the last vestige of so-called State sovereignty. He asserted that not one of the States had ever been a State out of the union—a point previously emphasized by Webster in his reply to Haynes. The original colonies became "free and independent States" in name only when the Declaration of Independence was signed. The union, he showed, had created the States. "Having never been States, either in substance or in name," he argued, "outside of the union, whence this magical omnipotence of 'State rights,' asserting a claim of power to lawfully destroy the union itself? Much is said about the 'sovereignty' of the States, but the word even is not in the national Constitution, nor, as is believed, in any of the State Constitutions. What is a 'sovereignty' in the political sense of the term? Would it be far wrong to define it 'a political community without a political superior?' Tested by this, no one of our States, except Texas, ever was a sovereignty, and even Texas gave up that character on coming into the union, by which act she acknowledged the Constitution of the United States and the laws and treaties of the United States made in pursuance of the Constitution to be for her the supreme law of the land."

This was new doctrine to be laid before the American people but the inevitable logic of circumstances compelled its acceptance. Lincoln gave force to his utterance by acts which, under any other conditions, would have led to his impeachment. He called for militia volunteers to serve for three years, and for large additions to the army and navy, without waiting for Congress to exercise a power under the Constitution; he issued a proclamation blockading the ports of the southern States; and, finally, because of disturbances in Maryland he directed the suspension of the writ of *habeas corpus* at any point of the military line between Philadelphia and Washington, a territory not in rebellion. Lincoln explained to Congress that "these measures, whether strictly legal or not, were ventured upon under what appeared to be a popular demand and a public necessity, trusting then, as now, that Congress would ratify them." He justified his action in suspending the writ of *habeas corpus,* also, on the ground that a dangerous emergency existed, although he expressed a doubt whether the power was vested in him or in Congress. Judge Taney, acting in the District Court, decided that his action was unconstitutional. Afterwards Congress, representing the people, stepped into the breach and exercised the authority to the extent of directing the suspension of the writ throughout the United States.

Every year of the war made the people more and more familiar with the omnipotence of the Federal government. They accepted, not altogether without mental reservation, the seizure of persons by Federal authorities in peaceful States, the prisoners being denied either the writ of *habeas corpus* or trial by jury. The provisions of the Constitution which guaranteed to the people that the right to be secure in their persons, houses, papers and effects, against unwarrantable searches and seizures, shall not be violated; which forbid arrest without warrant, and which assure each accused person "a speedy and public trial by an impartial jury," were daily disregarded. The so-called Confiscation Act, by which, through legislative enactment, millions of dollars' worth of property were declared forfeited, although a supplemental joint resolution provided that real estate forfeiture was not to extend beyond the natural life of the offenders who came within the provisions of the Act, was but one of the many examples of the extent to which the Federal government could and did go. Practical illustrations of the power of the Federal government were visible on every hand. There was not time to question or to reason. Throughout the whole length and breadth of the land there was universal acquiescence in the most extreme measures because it could not be otherwise. When it was treason to utter a thought which reflected upon the Federal government, the people learned to respect, if not always to love, the authority which that government exercised with unsparing hand. "Centralization," says Dunning, in his "Essays on the Civil War and Reconstruction," "was the order of the day. Conspicuous among the illustrations of this fact appear the substitution of a national for a State system of banking and currency; the creation of a national militia system to occupy the field once held by the State systems, and the sweeping jurisdiction conferred by the *Habeas Corpus Act* upon the national judiciary at the expense of the State courts."

Nor was this all. Through the fourteenth and fifteenth amendments to the Constitution the people were to learn that the States could be told what they could do and could not do respecting their citizens in the matter of equal enjoyment of privileges and immunities and the right to vote. In their provisions these amendments were far more definitive of the subordinate character of a State than any previous clause in the Constitution and they never could have been adopted if the Nation had not loomed large in the public mind. This same point of view tolerated strong measures by the Federal government in the reconstruction period and enabled proclamations to be issued and laws to be passed which would not have been possible before 1861. It is not within the province of this work to enter upon a political history of the war period, although the subject deserves adequate treatment, while the volumes on the military history form a library in themselves. Our present purpose is to emphasize the psychological effect upon the American people of witnessing demonstration after demonstration of the transcendent power of the Federal government. Amid the excitement and the peril which followed the fall of Sumter there was neither opportunity nor disposition to analyze too closely the acts of the President and of Congress; and later in the war the people became callous to the widest exercise of Federal authority. They realized that "the bundle of sticks" had become compressed under the stress of war into one compact piece of timber. The doctrine of State sovereignty had been literally re-cast in the fiery furnace. The people were permeated with the spirit of national union. It was not the governments at Springfield or Albany or Harrisburg, but the Government at Washington which still lived. The eyes of the nation were thereafter to be focused upon the national capital. The political entities of the States became overshadowed by the national feeling. The outlines of the Federal government, on the other hand, stood out against the horizon like the Parthenon on the Acropolis at Athens, distinct, commanding and supreme.

Chapter V

THE DOCTRINE OF PARAMOUNT NECESSITY

THE logical result of the convincing demonstration of Federal omnipotence soon became apparent. The people, through their duly elected Representatives, instinctively turned to the Federal government to secure the accomplishment of reforms which could not be reached in any other way. During the Civil War they had seen the Federal power exercised arbitrarily and sometimes harshly, but always effectively. This was the fact that impressed the American mind. It was the achievement of results by direct methods which appealed to the masses. The initiative toward the larger manifestation of Federal authority was now put forth by the people themselves.

The first reform which demanded attention was the substitution of a national banking system for the unsafe and troublesome operation of State banks. There was, of course, no authority in the

Constitution for the Federal government to go into the States and throttle these institutions but there was in the Constitution a provision which authorized the levying of taxes. What could not be done by direct means could be accomplished by indirection. It was only necessary to place a tax upon all State bank issues sufficiently high to render their circulation unprofitable and the deed was done. Such a law was enacted in 1864 and was upheld by the Supreme Court.

The extinction of State bank currency was accomplished so simply and so easily that quite naturally the people invoked the aid of the Federal power for the suppression of the lottery evil. Times had changed since Congress had authorized the holding of a government lottery in the District of Columbia and there was a loud demand for reform. Some attempt had been made by Congress to keep the tickets and literature of "illegal lotteries" out of the mails but the legislation had not been effective because the express as a means of transportation was still available, and because the lottery companies, in order to escape all interference, established themselves in contiguous Central American territory. Congress, therefore, in 1890 passed "an act for the suppression of the lottery traffic through national and interstate commerce and the postal service subject to the jurisdiction and laws of the United States." The law not only prohibited any person from bringing into the United States or depositing in the mails any lottery ticket or lottery advertisement but forbade these things from being carried "from one State to another." This was a novel conception of the extent of the power of the post office and was the first law which seemed to bear within its provisions the germ of apparent unconstitutional encroachment upon the police power of the States, this consideration being swept aside by the doctrine of paramount necessity. "The demand for the suppression of this lottery traffic comes from all sections of the country," said Representative Broderick, in charge of the bill, and after adding that "this lottery business has grown to such an extent that it has checked the moral sense of the people of the entire country," he had no other argument to offer. None was needed. If the people demanded it, it must be done. There was no serious debate upon the merits of the proposition from a constitutional point of view in either the Senate or the House and it became a law by a practically unanimous vote.

But what the people wanted and what the Constitution gave Congress the power to enact were widely different matters and the Supreme Court was called upon to adjudicate the question. The arrest of a man who shipped lottery tickets from Texas to California was contested upon the ground that the regulation of lotteries was wholly within the jurisdiction of the police power of the States. The Supreme Court in 1903 overruled this contention, deciding that lottery tickets were subjects of traffic and their transportation by common carriers from one State to another was interstate commerce which Congress might prohibit under its power to regulate commerce among the States. One sentence in the majority decision illustrates the principle which has been uppermost in sustaining all enlarged grants of Federal power. "As a State may, for the purpose of guarding the morals of its own people," said Justice Harlan, "forbid all sales of lottery tickets within its limits, so Congress, for the purpose of guarding the people of the United States against the 'widespread pestilence of lotteries' and to protect the commerce which concerns all the States"—which phrase seems to have been inserted as a secondary and saving clause—"may prohibit the carrying of lottery tickets from one State to another." This idea of paternally safeguarding the morals of the people through legislation which stretched the Constitution to its utmost limit—an idea which permeates present-day Congressional enactment—did not, however, meet with the approval of the entire court. As a matter of fact, the court was almost equally divided, five in the affirmative and four in the negative. Among the dissenters was Chief Justice Fuller, who characterized the opinion of the court as "a long step in the direction of wiping out all State lines and the creation of a centralized government." He differentiated between the moral and the legal aspect. "It will not do to say," he declared, "that State laws have been found to be ineffective for the suppression of lotteries, and, therefore, Congress should intervene. The scope of the commerce clause of the Constitution cannot be enlarged because of present views of public interest."

But even though it might be by the narrow majority of one, the lottery evil was blotted out by invoking Federal aid, which was the result desired, and the people did not care how close was the margin of strength so long as the victory was won. It was but natural, therefore, that upon the next occasion of public necessity the strong arm of the government should again be brought into requisition. In the year 1893 there was a menace of cholera and the suggestion of a national quarantine met with instant favor. It is an interesting fact in this connection, as showing how popular sentiment can change in a century, that in 1799 a law was passed by Congress directing Federal custom revenue officers "to duly observe the quarantine laws of any State and faithfully aid in their execution," while in 1898 Congress enacted a law which empowered and authorized State quarantine officers "to act as officers of the national quarantine system and shall be clothed with all the powers of United States officers for quarantine purposes." Herein was a complete reversal of the relative importance of State and Federal officers. When the Federal government was given full control of the quarantine system the law went so far as to authorize the Secretary of the Treasury, in the event that the quarantine regulations of any State or municipality were not, in his opinion, sufficient to prevent the introduction of infectious or contagious diseases from foreign countries, to promulgate rules and regulations which would supersede State law. This, indeed, was investing a Federal official with extensive power, but in this case, as in every other, the plea of necessity was successfully raised. The majority report in the House, submitted by Representative Rayner, a Maryland Democrat, insisted that it was "of the utmost importance that something should be done," and added:

> "Some of the States—but very few indeed—have ample and efficient quarantine regulations, while others have legislation upon the subject which is utterly impotent for the purpose for which it was designed, and still others have no statutes or provisions upon the subject at all. It is idle and useless to say that this is a matter that ought to be left to the conflicting laws of the different States. No one State has it within its power to protect itself from the importation of an epidemic."

In this brief paragraph, written little more than twenty years ago, is embodied the consideration which has had such a controlling influence upon the growth of Federal power. Some States have good legislation, others poor legislation, and still others no legislation at all. This is, apparently, good and sufficient reason why all the patchwork laws of the States should be superseded by a blanket statute enacted by the Federal Congress.

The argument is appealing and effective, even though, as when the quarantine law was under consideration, a few of the old-time faith utter their protest. There was something novel, at least, in the doctrine that a Federal official should make laws which would govern the States and that he was himself to be the judge of whether a State or municipal law was sufficient. It was pointed out that it might be possible for a Federal official in Washington to frame a code of laws which would restrain the personal liberty of a citizen of New Jersey returning from New York, even though his actions would be wholly legal according to State law, "and irrespective of the fact that he is in no way engaged in commerce." The bill was further criticized as "a long stride in the direction of Federal control of matters hitherto exclusively within the jurisdiction of the State," while the minority report, written by Mr. Mallory, of Florida, contained this caustic comment:

"On the plea of necessity the House of Representatives is asked once more to organize a raid upon State authority, to invade the sacred domain of personal liberty, to wrest from the local authorities of the States a power which up to this time has been exclusively theirs, and, in order to effectually secure these ends, to delegate to a single administrative officer its high legislative functions."

All of which was doubtless true, as well as the further comment that the Secretary of the Treasury was made a Supreme Court to decide upon the sufficiency of State laws. Protest was in vain. Even a previous opinion of the United States Supreme Court, as handed down by Associate Justice Davis, to the effect that "the power to establish quarantine laws rests with the States and has not been surrendered to the general government," was disregarded. A few stalwart champions of State rights stood like Leonidas at the pass of Thermopylæ, but over them rode rough-shod a large majority of the people's representatives. All their arguments and assertions faded away before the overwhelming common-sense of the counter-proposition that uniformity in quarantine service and regulation was essential to public safety and that this conformity, to say nothing of efficiency and authority, could not be obtained except by vesting complete control in the Federal government. It was a question of fact against theory and this is a practical age. The solid and substantial fact triumphed over a thin and almost obsolete idea.

The doctrine of paramount necessity was again

invoked for the extension of Federal authority in the protection of the people against impure food and drugs, a matter which might very properly be considered as wholly within the jurisdiction of the States. On June 30, 1906, an act was approved which made it a serious misdemeanor to ship from one State to another any misbranded or adulterated article of food or drugs. The standards by which these articles were to be judged were to be set forth in rules and regulations framed by three Federal officials, the Secretary of the Treasury, the Secretary of Agriculture and the Secretary of Commerce and Labor. The act gave the Bureau of Chemistry the right to examine specimens, provided for the confiscation of illegal articles, gave Federal courts jurisdiction over prosecutions and went into much detail as to the manner in which the law should be administered. Long before this, in 1891, the Senate had passed a bill which looked toward securing purity of food and drugs, and in 1902 a law was enacted which authorized the Secretary of Agriculture "to establish standards of food and food products and determine what are regarded as adulterations therein for the guidance of the officials of the various States and the courts of justice." This law was so palpably within the domain of Congress as to excite no comment. Under it certain standards were duly proclaimed and some of the States passed laws in conformity therewith. It did not, however, prevent fraud from being practiced upon the people and the advocates of governmental control saw another opportunity to extend Federal authority. The present law was then prepared and introduced in Congress. The report which accompanied the bill in the Senate was brief and perfunctory, embracing only two sentences, with neither reason nor argument for the proposed legislation. In the House the majority report brought forward the familiar plea. "We believe," it asserted, "that every one recognizes the necessity of governmental regulation to prevent the sale of adulterated, poisonous or other injurious food products." The statement was frankly made that the object of the proposed law "is to obtain uniformity of food standards among the States," and then the report, again emphasizing the word "necessity," continued:

"The necessity for pure food laws is apparent to every one. Many of the States have endeavored to meet this necessity as far as they can, but the several States have proven unable to fully deal with the matter when affected by interstate commerce in adulterated and misbranded articles. . . . The laws and regulations of the different States are divers, confusing and often contradictory."

Very able and comprehensive—but also very ineffective—were the arguments in opposition to the measure. It was contended that "the power of government to regulate the sale of food products and drugs, prohibit adulteration of the same, prescribe the manner in which they shall be branded and fix the size and weight of the packages in which such food products and drugs shall be contained, is admittedly an exercise of police power," and, therefore, not within the jurisdiction of Congress. The belief was expressed that the legislatures of the several States had full power and authority to enact such laws and protect the people of the States. It was further claimed that the States had enacted these laws and were enforcing them. The broad principle was laid down that "the power to protect the people of the various States in health, in morals and general welfare is inherent in the States—was reserved to the States by the Constitution, was not delegated to the Congress of the United States, and remains there to be exercised by the States at the will and pleasure of the legislatures of such States." Emphasis was laid upon the decision of the United States Supreme Court in the case of Plumley *vs.* Massachusetts (115 U. S. 461), which sustained the exclusive right of the State to pass and enforce laws for the protection of the health and morals of its people and to prevent the sale of articles of food manufactured in or brought from another State. Finally, the right of Congress to enact the proposed legislation was challenged and Congress was urged "to leave to the legislatures of the various States the duty of protecting the people of the States."

Both challenge and appeal were in vain. As against grave questions of constitutionality came this pathetic plea—literally the last words spoken in the debate:

> "I trust no member of this House will so far forget the good of his constituents as to vote against this bill."

In response to this all-persuasive argument the House passed the measure by a vote of 243 to 17. The vote in the Senate was 63 to 4. Thus was the Pure Food Law enacted—a law which has immeasurably stimulated the idea of the supremacy of the Federal government. Section 9 of the statute releases from the danger of prosecution any retail dealer who has the guarantee of a manufacturer, wholesaler or jobber that the articles furnished him are not misbranded or adulterated. The consequence is that nearly every manufactured article of food which now enters the household bears the magic legend, "Guaranteed under U. S. Pure Food Law," while the advertisements in newspapers and street cars assure the would-be purchaser that pickles and shrimps and catsup and herring bear the seal of Federal approval. No one can estimate the psychological effect which this constant reiteration has upon the public mind. It has accustomed millions of people to regard the Federal government as the personal protector of their welfare and has led them to invite further exercise of Federal power.

Chapter VI

FEDERAL CONTROL OVER RAILROADS AND TRUSTS

THE old proverb that fire is a good servant but a bad master became, as the country developed, particularly applicable to the railroads. The transportation lines had knit together the widely separated sections of the United States and, with the telegraph, had inspired the American people with a sense of unity. They were, in themselves, the very essence of the spirit of Federalism. They made the boundaries of the States of no importance. Under conditions of speed and comfort the traveler from the east to the west or from the north to the south paid no heed to the States traversed during his journey. It was the United States as one vast and solidified country which impressed itself upon his mind and this became especially true when the trans-continental roads linked the Atlantic and Pacific coasts with bands of steel. As the country grew, however, the railroads waxed in power. The corporations which owned them fondly imagined that they were beyond control and indulged in practices which were manifestly injurious to those who did not possess the influence to compel fair treatment. When this condition arose some of the States attempted remedial measures, either through the creation of railroad commissions or the enactment of laws which could only be effective within State boundaries. The so-called Granger movement in the middle west in the early 80's was an expression of resentment against railroad domination; but the reforms which this popular uprising succeeded in accomplishing were necessarily restricted. It was evident that this new menace to the public welfare could not be held in restraint except through the exercise of Federal power, nor was there any method whereby this authority could be brought into play except through the enactment of a Federal law.

Congress approached the subject with much care and deliberation. There was no doubt as to the necessity for action. Complaints against the railroads were numerous, beginning with the assertion that local rates were unreasonably high, as compared with through rates, and ending with charges of wasteful and extravagant management, with the consequent imposition of a needless tax upon the shipping and traveling public. The paramount evil was the unjust discrimination between persons and places in the matter of freight and passenger tolls. While there was no question as to the prevalence of unsatisfactory conditions, there was much hesitation as to the methods by which they were to be remedied and still more uncertainty as to the extent of the authority which Congress might exercise in the premises. Many months were spent in inquiry, the result being a recommendation that a commission be created which should be invested with Federal control of all the railroads in the United States. This was thirty years ago, at which time it was necessary to argue at considerable length in favor of the now universally conceded principle that the regulation of interstate commerce, even to the extent of fixing rates and traffic schedules, is a Federal function. At that time, too, there were railroad commissions in some twenty States which were struggling with the problem of railroad regulation, but investigation proved that their duties were mainly advisory and their recommendations generally ineffective. This made some plan of

Federal control absolutely necessary. It was formulated none too soon. Thirty years ago there were only 121,000 miles of railroad in the United States, which had been constructed at a gross cost of $5,000,000,000. To-day there are 264,378 miles of railroad, with nearly 2,500 separate corporations representing a capitalization of over $21,000,000,000 and employing 1,409,000 people. The enormous power wielded by this aggregrate of wealth could not have been controlled by the diverse legislation of individual States. Nothing less than a compact law, enforced by the strength of the Federal government, could have held it in restraint.

Since the first Interstate Commerce Commission law was passed in 1887 it has been frequently amended; but each addition has increased, instead of decreased, the power conferred upon the agents of the Federal government. More than once the argument has been made that the constitutional authority given to Congress to regulate commerce among the States could not be delegated to a commission, and that regulations promulgated by such a commission could not take the place of laws enacted by Congress. The argument has fallen upon deaf ears. It was evident that Congress could not give time to the consideration of the multitudinous details affecting railroad traffic, besides which the danger which threatened was so imminent that there was no patience with those who would split hairs over a technical construction of the Constitution. The report of the Senate committee, upon which the Interstate Commerce Commission bill was based, stated truthfully that "no general question of governmental policy occupies at this time so prominent a place in the minds of the people as that of controlling the steady growth and extending influence of corporate power and of regulating its relations to the public, and there are no corporations," it was added, "so directly connected with the public as the railroads." Pooling and rebates had already grown to be nation-wide evils. Each railroad corporation was a law unto itself and as it grew in extent and wealth and influence, it became more and more callous as to the public welfare. Expensive lobbies were maintained in each State capital to thwart antagonistic legislation or advocate selfish propositions. Passes were distributed freely as an insidious form of influence, and there was no hesitation in the use of still more objectionable methods of obtaining requisite votes.

To-day the railroad corporations, once so haughty and independent, bow in complete submission to Federal power, first exemplified in the Interstate Commerce Commission and now concentrated in the Director General of Railroads. In the early days of Federal supervision a few State legislatures attempted to preserve a semblance of jurisdiction by fixing the maximum rate to be charged within State boundaries, but as intrastate railroads are of minor importance, the legislation was necessarily limited in the extent of its application. Under war conditions the existence of the State is no longer considered. Federal control is complete. Even before the government took over the roads, however, the Interstate Commerce Commission had developed into one of the most important bureaus of the Federal system, costing over $1,000,000 annually to maintain. The practically unlimited jurisdiction conferred by Congress upon the Commission transferred the activities of railroad officials from the State capitals to the national capital, but reprehensible methods were no longer in vogue. There was a vast difference between dealing with widely separated and obscure State legislators on the one hand, and, upon the other hand, with Interstate Commerce

Commissioners, and, at present, a Director General of Railroads, appointed by the President and typifying the embodiment of Federal power. These officials can and do regulate and govern the railroads, not only in reducing or increasing rates within vast territory embracing many States, but in important matters of finance and administration. The present system of governmental control is, as yet, largely experimental; but even before we declared war against Germany, the American people were so thoroughly convinced that they had acted wisely in giving the Federal Commission plenary authority that when the Commerce Court, created for the purpose of reviewing the findings and orders of the Commission, rendered some judgments nullifying the work of the Commission, the demand for the abolition of the Court became too insistent for Congress to withstand. This expression of confidence in the Interstate Commerce Commission was but another expression of popular satisfaction with Federal control. The result which was sought for has been achieved. The subordination of the railroad corporations to Federal authority is now a finality; and if the results shall be advantageous—although this is not yet certain—the minds of the people will be strengthened in the belief that Federal power is a beneficent thing. The progress of the years is shown by the fact that the agency which did so much to inculcate the Federal spirit by the practical obliteration of State boundaries is now brought conclusively under Federal control.

Nor was railroad domination the only danger with which the legislatures of the States could not successfully cope. The great commercial development of the country had resulted in the formation of monopolistic combinations, popularly known as trusts. Some of these huge corporations practically controlled the entire field of the industry in which they operated. The Standard Oil Trust, for instance, "manufactured more than three-fourths of all the petroleum refined in the United States, marketed more than four-fifths of all the illuminating oil sold in the United States or exported from the United States, sold more than four-fifths of all the naphtha sold in the United States, and sold more than nine-tenths of all the lubricating oil purchased by railroad companies in the United States." The Sugar Trust, the Tobacco Trust, the Harvester Trust, the Steel Trust, the Copper Trust,—all these, and literally hundreds of other monopolies, were formed, stifling competition, fixing prices, and, in too many instances, controlling legislatures in opposition to public welfare. It was evident, long before all these Trusts had been organized, that the Federal power must be invoked to regulate and control them. There was not a whisper of the rights of the States, therefore, when the Sherman Anti-trust bill was under consideration in the Senate in 1890. The situation was too serious to be further jeopardized by the interposition of State rights doctrine. On the contrary, it was accepted that if the proposed law made illegal "every contract, combination in the form of trust or otherwise, or conspiracy in restraint of trade or commerce among the several States, or with foreign nations," it was plainly within the constitutional prerogative of Congress. Senator Sherman sounded the keynote which has inspired all legislation extending Federal power when he said:

"While we should not stretch the powers granted to Congress by strained construction, we cannot surrender any of them; they are not ours to surrender; but whenever occasion calls, we should exercise them for the benefit and protection of the people of the United States. And while I have no doubt that every word of this bill is within the powers granted to Congress, I feel that its defects are moderation, and that its best effect will be a warning that all trade and commerce, all agreements and arrangements, all struggles for money or property, must be governed by the universal law that the public good must be the test of all."

"For the benefit and protection of the people of the United States," and "the universal law that the public good must be the test of all." In these two pregnant phrases are summed up the Alpha and Omega of the persistent and unchecked extension of Federal power, even though the Constitution is strained thereby. The Senate was, in the old régime, generally supposed to be the refuge of the corporate interests; and yet when the anti-trust measure came to a vote Senator Blodgett, of New Jersey, had the unenviable distinction of being the only Senator recorded in the negative. The sentiment of the Senate was expressed most forcibly by Mr. Edmunds, of Vermont, Chairman of the Judiciary Committee, when he said that he was "in favor, most earnestly in favor, of doing anything that the Constitution of the United States has given Congress the power to do, to repress, and break up, and destroy forever the monopolies" of the character of the

Sugar Trust and the Oil Trust, "because in the long run," he added, "they are destructive of the public welfare, and come to be tyrannies, grinding tyrannies." With these views uttered in the Senate, and finding their endorsement in a practically unanimous vote, it was no wonder that the House of Representatives speedily and affirmatively acted and thus interposed the Federal power between almost omnipotent monopolies and a defenseless people. It is true that it has required many years of tedious litigation to establish the law. The corporations did not surrender their tremendous advantage without a struggle. Eventually, however, the Sugar Trust, the Oil Trust and the Tobacco Trust were compelled to dissolve, while other combinations, facing the inevitable, voluntarily consented to take the action which, in due course of time, the courts would have directed.

For nearly a quarter of a century the law remained in effect, undergoing constantly broadening interpretation in the courts. It was evident, however, that there were loopholes which had not been closed, and the passage of the so-called Clayton Act, approved October 14, 1914, placed further obstacles in the way of creation of monopolies. For instance, price discrimination, "tying contracts," holding companies and interlocking directorates—all of which were utilized by unscrupulous corporations to substantially lessen competition—were prohibited under heavy penalties. Even this drastic law did not, however, meet every situation and in the Federal Trade Commission Act of September 26, 1914, the Federal government was given power to deeply probe into the conduct of business. In this law there is recognition of the fact that unfair methods of competition prevail in the commercial world and means are provided for remedying the evil. Power to execute the provisions of the act is conferred upon five Commissioners appointed by the President and confirmed by the Senate and the authority is of the broadest character. Action may be instituted "whenever the commission shall have reason to believe that any such person, partnership or corporation has been or is using any unfair method of competition in commerce." The commission is also empowered to require, by general or special orders, corporations engaged in commerce, excepting banks and common carriers subject to the act to regulate commerce, to furnish to the commission in writing such information respecting their organization, business, conduct, practices and management as may be required. More than this, the commission is accorded the legal right to make public such information, except trade secrets and names of customers, if such publication is deemed expedient. In the measure as originally drafted it was gravely proposed that Federal agents should at all times have the right to violate the privacy of any corporation doing an interstate business to the extent of inspecting its books and records and could also publish the result of its investigation. In the law as finally enacted this provision is somewhat restricted in that the right of examination is limited to those corporations which are being investigated or have been proceeded against, but none the less we have now reached the point where Federal agents can become acquainted with the innermost details of corporate existence and can, if they so desire, publish their knowledge to the business world. No corporation is safe from Federal investigation because there is no manufacturing or other industry worthy of the name whose goods do not pass across State lines.

It has been suggested that corporations may find protection against unprovoked Federal inquisition in the security which is guaranteed by the

Constitution "against unreasonable searches and seizures" of persons, houses, papers and effects. It is extremely doubtful whether this contention will hold. The Supreme Court of the United States is not likely to decide that an examination conducted for the public good into the affairs of a corporation is "unreasonable," even though no law has been violated by the corporation. The fact that Congress has authorized such examination, that Federal officers are executing the law and that the burden of proving innocence rests by common consent upon the corporation, renders it easy to predict that this particular form of the exercise of Federal power will not be modified in the slightest degree.

While the Federal government has not yet attempted to compel the settlement of disputes between common carriers engaged in interstate transportation and their employees engaged in train operation or train service, it has created a Board of Mediation and Conciliation, under the act of July 15, 1913, to settle by mediation, conciliation and arbitration controversies concerning wages, hours of labor or conditions of employment. Whenever such controversy arises and interrupts or threatens to interrupt the operation of trains to the serious detriment of the public interest, the Board of Mediation may offer its services to bring about an agreement or, upon the request of either party, is required to use its best efforts by mediation and conciliation to the same end. If an amicable adjustment cannot be secured, the Board endeavors to induce the parties to submit their dispute to arbitration, and, if successful, makes the necessary arrangements for such arbitration. There have been numerous instances of attempted mediation and while they have not always been successful, the results have fully warranted the enactment of the law. All that is now lacking, in the view of the advocates of absolute Federal control, is compulsory obedience to the mandates of the Board and it is not unlikely that this omission will be supplied. The doctrine of paramount necessity will be invoked and then the Federal power will again protect the people against the undue prolongation of disputes which operate against the public interests.

Chapter VII

THE FEDERAL POWER AND THE PEOPLE

THE extension of the power and authority of the Federal government has been erroneously characterized as Federal usurpation. The dictionary definition of the word "usurpation" is "the act of seizing, or occupying and enjoying, the place, power, functions or property of another without right." This is not the situation as it exists in the United States to-day. Power and functions have been thrust upon executive officers, the visible impersonations of the Federal government, by the representatives of the people in Congress assembled. Hamilton very properly observed, in the "Federalist" papers, that the fabric of the American empire ought to rest upon the solid basis of the consent of the people; and if the people consent to grant large powers to the Federal government, those powers are legitimate and are not usurped.

It has already been shown that much of the

Federal legislation enacted by Congress was based upon the doctrine of paramount necessity. This has not been, however, the only inspiring cause. There has been in the minds of the people an instinct, selfish though it might be, which has led them to gain for themselves all possible advantage through the extension of governmental functions. No one can analyze the appropriations made by Congress without being impressed by the fact that the people, through their representatives, have insisted upon the Federal revenues being diverted into channels which would insure the greatest good to the greatest number. Even Thomas Jefferson, stalwart opponent of Federalism as he was, could not resist the temptation offered by a surplus in the treasury in 1806, and suggested that the money be applied to "the great purposes of public education, roads, rivers, canals, and such other objects of public improvement as it may be thought proper." He doubted, however, the authority of Congress thus to dispose of the Federal funds and recommended an appropriate amendment to the Constitution. President Madison also called the attention of Congress to "the great importance of establishing throughout our country the roads and canals which can best be executed under National authority," and while he lauded the efforts of the States, pointed out that "National jurisdiction and National means" would be more effective. He recognized, as Jefferson did, a constitutional defect against carrying his program into effect, and later vetoed a bill which had passed Congress to use Federal funds for internal improvements, holding that the power to regulate commerce did not include the power to construct roads and canals, nor improve the navigation of watercourses. He expressed the belief, also, "that the permanent success of the Constitution depends upon a definite partition of powers between the General and the State Governments." President Monroe vetoed in 1822, upon the same grounds, "An act for the preservation and repair of the Cumberland Road"; in 1830 President Jackson vetoed the Maysville Turnpike bill, the first of a series of vetoes of internal improvement bills; and as late as 1847 President Polk vetoed a river and harbor bill. The men in Congress who shared these views introduced amendments to the Constitution by which they sought to fairly confer upon Congress the power which seemed to be a matter of doubt.

No concerted effort was, however, put forth toward securing the adoption of these proposed amendments and, in the meantime, the door of the Federal treasury stood invitingly open. The desire to benefit from the expenditure of Federal funds overcame all scruples. A popular pressure which could not be withstood finally led Congress to embark upon a policy which, up to the present time, has resulted in the expenditure of nearly $1,000,000,000 for river and harbor improvements alone. It has not been unusual for appropriation bills of this character to aggregate as much as $80,000,000 in a single year and for the enjoyment of participating in the distribution of this vast amount of Federal wealth, the States eagerly welcome the presence of Federal agents within their boundaries and hasten to demonstrate the navigability of streams which are only deep enough to float barges and logs. The construction of public buildings has been another favorite method of securing the expenditure of Federal funds within State borders, only a few brave and conscientious spirits questioning the honesty of wholesale raids upon the National Treasury. The point to be emphasized, however, is that the idea of legitimatizing these appropriations by the adoption of an amendment to the Constitution has been utterly forgotten, because if the people's representatives decide that these expenditures are to be made, who shall say them nay?

A well-filled Federal treasury invites a multitude of appropriations. It is the money of the people, and the representatives of the people spend it for their constituents. Who are these constituents? The rural population of the United States, according to the last census, was over 48,000,000; of whom 25,000,000 were males, while the urban was only 42,000,000. In the fact that a majority of the electorate of this country resides in rural districts is to be found the convincing reason for the extension of governmental functions in behalf of the agriculturist. The golden bait of getting something for nothing is dangled before the eyes of the farmers by vote-seeking Congressmen and the farmers, in turn, quite willingly forget the duties which the State owes to its citizens as they share in the benefits of Federal activities. The Department of Agriculture, which is the executive division of the government most intimately connected with the farming class, has developed with hot-house rapidity under the nurture of Federalistic sentiment. The figures tell the story. In 1894, the division of botany in the Department of Agriculture cost $8,600 per annum, while twenty years later the appropriations for the Bureau of Plant Industry aggregated over $2,000,000. The expenditures of the Bureau of Forestry increased during the same period from $7,280 to considerably in excess of $5,000,000. The Bureau of Chemistry is comparatively a new creation, but this does not prevent it from spending over $1,000,000 a year, mainly for the enforcement of the pure food law. Meat inspection, a responsibility from which the States have been relieved, also costs $1,000,000 annually. Consideration for the welfare of the people is undoubtedly within the sphere of government, but it is certain that the founders of this republic never contemplated the degree of intimate regard for the individual which is now apparent. The vast sums expended by Federal agents concern every detail of farm life—not only as to advising the farmer as to the care of his animals and plants, including ornamental shrubs, and an inquiry into the diseases of ginseng, but how to bale and wrap his cotton, cure his tobacco and market his eggs. We have certainly reached a remarkable stage in our national existence when a Southern Democrat can announce upon the floor of the House, with apparent satisfaction, that "five hundred and thirty-five hog pastures were built in Georgia under the plan of the Federal Department of Agriculture."

Another striking instance of bureaucratic growth is the Bureau of Standards. In its inception, a little more than twenty years ago, this office consisted of an adjuster, a mechanician, a messenger and a watchman. To-day this Bureau expends nearly one million dollars per annum, is housed in costly buildings surrounded by extensive grounds, and its duties range from investigating the danger to life and property due to the transmission of electric currents at high potentials, to determining the fire-resisting properties of building materials. The people, through Congress, have granted these large sums and authorized these unusual governmental duties on the theory, apparently, that the work is for the public welfare and cannot, or will not, be undertaken by the States. Certainly no other reason can be advanced, for instance, for taking out of the Federal treasury $400,000 in a single year for the sole purpose of eradicating the cattle tick. The most notable advance in recent years, however, is in the rural free delivery mail service. Nobody questions the fact that postal matters are within the jurisdiction of the Federal government but this one item demonstrates how great a single branch of public service can become. In the post office appropriation bill for 1894 appears a modest appropriation of $10,000 to be applied, under the direction of the Postmaster General, to experimental free delivery in rural communities other than towns and villages. The post office appropriation bill for the current year carries for this experiment of two decades ago the enormous sum of nearly $55,000,000.

So enlarged have the powers and duties of the Federal government become that the Civil Service Commission, which in 1894 consisted of three Commissioners and a dozen clerks, is now a most pretentious Bureau, requiring several hundred clerks and a large executive staff to handle the examination papers of the army of government employees. The field force of the Commission alone to-day costs more than the entire expense of the organization in 1894. The enforced growth of the Federal power also creates a constant demand for new Departments. Two have been established in recent years, the latest being the Department of Labor, while a Department of Health is being earnestly advocated. These Departments naturally increase the number of Bureaus. In the Department of Commerce, a comparatively new institution, there are the Bureau of Corporations, the Bureau of Lighthouses, the Bureau of Foreign and Domestic Commerce, the Bureau of Fisheries, the Bureau of Navigation, the Bureau of Mines and several others. There are scores upon scores of Bureaus in connection with the eleven Departments of the Government, and Government inspectors or officials of various kinds now number thousands where, a few years ago, they could be counted by the score. In view of this, it is impossible not to recall the fact that one of the complaints against King George III in the Declaration of Independence was in these words:

"He has erected a multitude of new offices, and sent thither swarms of officers, to harass our people and eat out our substance."

What is to be said to-day, when a multitude of new offices is being erected every year and when swarms of officers are maintained at enormous cost upon the public treasury? Of course, in the days of our forefathers, the objectionable officers were imposed upon the people by a monarch against their will. To-day the offices are created by laws enacted by the representatives of the people, the latter being now quite willing to be harassed and to allow their substance to go into the pockets of Federal officials.

The end is not yet. It is practically certain, for example, that within the next ten years the Bureau of Education, now a modest attachment of the Department of the Interior, will reach colossal size. There is in Congress a growing belief that the dispensing of education in wholesale fashion is a governmental duty, without regard to the efforts put forth, or the facilities provided by, the States. It is true that the House of Representatives, after an entire day spent in debate, declined to pass a measure which directed the Commissioner of Education to investigate illiteracy among the adult population of the United States and report upon the means by which this illiteracy might be reduced or eliminated; but defeat was only made possible by the opposing influence of the all-powerful chairman of the Committee on Appropriations, Mr. Fitzgerald, of New York, who protested against "a movement which, if continued and not stopped, means an entire change in our system of government, a practical subordination of State and local governments, if not the elimination of local self-government in this country, and the building up of a great Federalized central government, which I believe is the greatest menace to this country."

The defeat of this particular measure did not dishearten those who, despite Mr. Fitzgerald's warning, would indefinitely extend governmental activities. On February 23, 1917, the Federal Board of Vocational Education was established. The law approved on that date provided for appropriations eventually aggregating $6,000,000 annually "to be paid to the respective States for the purpose of coöperating with the States in paying the salaries of teachers, supervisors, and directors of agricultural subjects, and teachers of trade, home economics and industrial subjects, and in the preparation of teachers of agricultural, trade, industrial and home economic subjects." It is further stipulated that any State, in order to secure the benefit of appropriations, shall, through its legislative authority, accept the provisions of the act and designate a State board to coöperate with the Federal Board. Upon the latter is imposed the duty "to make or cause to have made studies, investigations, and reports, with particular reference to their use in aiding the States in the establishment of vocational schools and classes and in giving instruction in agriculture, trades and industries, commerce and commercial pursuits, and home economics. Such studies, investigations, and reports shall include agriculture and agricultural processes and requirements upon agricultural workers; trades, industries, and apprenticeships, trade and industrial requirements upon industrial workers, and classification of industrial processes and pursuits; commerce and commercial pursuits and requirements upon commercial workers; home management, domestic science, and the study of related facts and principles; and problems of administration of vocational schools and of courses of study and instruction in vocational subjects."

This broadening of the field of Federal work would seem to be all-embracing, but it is only the entering wedge. The Commissioner of Education now seriously proposes that Congress shall place at his disposal a sum eventually aggregating $22,000,000 a year in order to provide physical education, $20,000,000 to be used, in coöperation with the States, in paying the salaries of directors, supervisors and teachers employed in the work. The scope of this new Federal activity is fully presented in Section 2 of the proposed law which reads as follows:

"The purpose and aim of physical education in the meaning of this Act shall be; more fully and thoroughly to prepare the boys and girls of the nation for the duties and responsibilities of citizenship through the development of bodily vigor and endurance, muscular strength and skill, bodily and mental poise and such desirable moral and social qualities as courage, self-control, self-subordination and obedience to authority, coöperation under leadership, and disciplined initiative; through adequate physical examination and the correction of postural and other remediable defects; through promotion of hygienic school and home life; and through scientific sanitation of school buildings, playgrounds and athletic fields and equipment thereof."

It has also been suggested that the Federal government undertake a general education survey of the United States and its possessions, although the author of the measure, with a qualm of State right's conscience, is willing to have States and localities bear half the expense when they coöperate with the Federal Commissioner of Education. Many other educational schemes have been introduced in Congress—the establishment of an elementary industrial school in the Appalachian mountains and the creation of educational parental courts, for instance,—and the number is certain to be increased in the near future. It is a conservative prediction to say that some of them will be enacted into laws. If the Federal government can go into the States to afford aid to the individual farmer; if it can insure the purity of every article of food manufactured within a State border; if it can carry our parcels and take care of our surplus earnings, it can certainly undertake universal education. The argument of the greatest good to the greatest number, regardless of Constitutional limitations or State jurisdiction, will prevail in the future as it has in the past. Very extravagant may seem the propositions just cited, but they are not more so than actual laws and appropriations recently enacted, and the scope of which, ten or twenty years ago, would have been regarded as beyond imagination.

There is one phase of Federal power, which, although granted by the people through their representatives, is still, in the minds of many, open to serious question. This is the reservation for future use of enormous tracts of land in the western States. The law which empowers the President to set apart "public lands wholly or in part covered with undergrowth, whether of commercial value or not, as public reservations," was, at first, administered in restricted fashion; but, during Roosevelt's administration, the principle of conservation was carried by him to such a degree that Congress passed a law forbidding further forest reservations to be made in Colorado, Wyoming, Idaho, Montana, Washington or Oregon, without its consent. President Roosevelt, aware that this prohibition would pass Congress, circumvented its purpose by reserving additional areas aggregating 30,000,000 acres during the ten days intervening after the Congressional enactment had been presented to him for approval. There have now been withdrawn 192,000,000 acres under the Forest Reserve Act, and numerous forest rangers and other Federal agents now appear in the western country and compel obedience to Federal regulations. Under laws enacted by the representatives of the people the imposition upon the western States has gone much further. Various statutes, which need not be recited in detail, tax the natural resources of the public domain through leases of grazing, oil, phosphate, asphaltum, coal and mineral lands for the benefit of the Federal treasury, while power plants are made to pay a royalty to the Federal government for each horse-power generated by falling water. In Colorado no less than 15,000,000 acres of land have been set aside as forest reserves, while 10,000,000 acres of coal land have been withdrawn from entry or a leasing value set upon them so high as to make their utilization prohibitive. This vast territory is equal to the area covered by the entire States of Massachusetts, Connecticut, New Hampshire and Rhode Island. In Oregon over 16,000,000 acres and in Washington more than 10,000,000 acres are under Federal dominion, with no possibility of the States enjoying the benefit therefrom.

The attitude of these States is naturally one of protest against alleged injustice. Their citizens point to the acts which enabled them to form a State government and which provided that "the State, when formed, shall be admitted into the Union upon an equal footing with the original States in all respects whatever," and claim a violation of those statutes because the advantages possessed by the original States have been denied to them. Not only has the growth of population been greatly retarded by making settlement difficult and restricting the area for home-builders to occupy, but, inasmuch as no taxes can be collected upon lands owned by the United States, the revenue, as well as the resources of the States, have been seriously impaired. It is pointed out, for instance, that the natural resources of Pennsylvania are not taxed by the Federal government, but accrue to the benefit of the State and its citizens, whereas in the western States they are a source of Federal profit. It is no wonder that in States where the Federal government exercises so much control there is a feeling of resentment, or that the assertion that these conditions represent a degree of interference in local affairs never before attempted in this country finds a responsive echo within their borders.

Chapter VIII

BROADENING THE FEDERAL FIELD

WHEN experiments had become experiences, the area of Federal control broadened with tremendous rapidity. A flood of Federal legislation descended upon the country, sweeping everything before it. With breadth and impetus the flood has now swept over the intervening State barriers and is still moving onward with irresistible force.

These enactments have come as the logical outcome of events. The public mind has become completely saturated with a feeling of absolute faith in the efficacy of Federal power. Propositions that a few years ago would have been ridiculed are now accepted with composure and even cordiality, the mastery attained over railroad and other corporations having whetted the public appetite for further conquests. Naturally there was no hesitation when, in response to an imperative demand, the suggestion was made that the

Federal power might be successfully employed in suppressing the traffic in women for immoral purposes. The so-called White Slave Act is an attempt on the part of the Federal government to lessen immorality by burdening vice with conditions and punishments which make its practice difficult. The statute was an evolution. As long ago as 1875 a Federal act made it illegal to import women for immoral purposes, but not being wholly effective, another law was passed in 1907. As this contained an unconstitutional provision, it was later amended. It did not remedy the evil. There was still a traffic in women which neither Federal nor State law had been able to reach. Once again, therefore, the Federal power was called into requisition and by an ingenious scheme the reform was accomplished under the comprehensive authority given to Congress to regulate commerce among the several States. The act, as finally approved, forbids the transporting, or obtaining transportation for, in interstate or foreign commerce, any woman or girl for the purpose of prostitution or debauchery, or for any other immoral purpose; and the Supreme Court has already decided that the transportation need not be in or by an interstate carrier. Persuading, inducing, enticing or coercing any woman or girl to go from one State to another for acts thus made illegal is prohibited under heavy penalties.

The law, however, goes still further. It embraces intent or purpose in connection with transportation of women and girls for immoral purposes. This section of the law was severely criticized as bringing a purely mental operation under the domain of interstate commerce; and it was also questioned whether conversation could be regarded as being within the meaning of the word "commerce" in the Constitution. On the other hand, it was argued that if the transportation of lottery tickets could be prohibited, not because pieces of paper were in themselves harmful, but because of the injurious connection between them and the entire scheme of the lottery, the interstate transportation of women for the purposes of immorality could also be made illegal. It was shown, too, that the Supreme Court had held that solicitation of business for a firm outside of its own State was a part of interstate commerce. It was not the arguments as to the constitutionality of the proposed law, however, which determined its enactment. It was the fact that the so-called White Slave traffic "shocked the moral sense of the nation," and the people, through their representatives, were bent upon its abolition, even if the power of the Federal Government had to be invoked in devious ways. The fact that the United States Supreme Court has upheld the law in at least four decisions will further stimulate the exercise of the Federal power in overcoming the next evil which arouses nation-wide condemnation.

Not only do men and women crossing State borders pass under the control of the Federal Government, but even the birds that fly through the air have been placed in the same category. In a law approved March 3, 1913, making appropriations for the Department of Agriculture, is a clause which declares that all migratory and insectivorous birds which do not remain permanently throughout the entire year in any State or Territory, "shall hereafter be deemed within the custody and protection of the Government of the United States, and shall not be destroyed or taken contrary to regulations hereinafter provided for." These regulations are to be promulgated by the Department of Agriculture, and fine or imprisonment is to be the punishment of any person convicted of their violation. A provision in the law, not devoid of sarcastic humor, asserts "that nothing herein contained shall be deemed . . . to prevent the States and Territories from enacting laws and regulations to promote and render efficient the regulations of the Department of Agriculture provided under this act." In other words, the moment the President of the United States made this statute effective by affixing his signature of approval, that moment all provisions of the game laws of all the States which were in conflict with a series of regulations framed by a Federal official at Washington were wiped out of existence. So completely has the Federal authority supplanted the authority of the States in this particular that recently, when citizens and land-owners in South Carolina desired to shoot ducks in that State during a certain month, they were compelled to confer with the Chief of the Biological Survey in Washington, an appointed official paid a salary of $3,500 a year, in order to obtain the necessary permission, even though the season in which they desired to indulge in the sport was legal according to their State laws.

Two reasons seem to have actuated the representatives of the people in Congress in this complete surrender of State sovereignty—first, that unless birds are safe-guarded the injury done by insects will increase and that this protection could not be accorded except by the Federal Government owing to "the multiplicity of State laws and the divergence of their provisions." The profundity of the argument brought to bear upon the Senate is shown in the favorable report made to that body upon the bill. "But for the vegetation the insects would perish," it says, "and but for the insects the birds would perish, and but for the birds the vegetation would be utterly destroyed." Thus were rhythm and logic happily combined; while it was also soberly quoted in the debate, as another reason for a Federal law, that although Texas makes the killing of a robin an offense punishable by a fine of $5, the law is not enforced by the State, wherefore the heavy hand of Federal authority must be laid not only upon Texas but upon every other State in the Union. As against such arguments as these, the serious presentation of State jurisdiction under the Constitution was naturally unavailing. In vain was it urged that the blackbird or the goose that wings its flight across the blue vault of heaven has neither consignor nor consignee, and is not, therefore, interstate commerce; or that the Federal Government has no police power in the States for the protection of its property not on Federal ground; or that it was preposterous to suppose that a barefoot boy could be arrested, taken before a Federal judge, and fined or imprisoned for an act which was not in violation of any local statute. Judicial determination of the Constitutionality of this act is now pending in the United States Supreme Court in the case of the United States, plaintiff in error, *vs.* Harvey C. Shauver; but, in the meantime, Congress has re-affirmed the law and has made it operative by granting to the Federal Government a generous appropriation for its enforcement. It is not surprising that an effort is now being made to place migratory fishes under Federal control, so that even the Mississippi catfish may erelong swim proudly under government protection.

Another striking and most unusual instance of the exercise of Federal power was presented in the Congressional investigations of purely local strike conditions in West Virginia, Michigan and Colorado. It will be remembered that President Cleveland directed United States troops to be employed in an effort, during the strike of railroad employees in Chicago, to insure the safe and uninterrupted transit of the United States mail, the local authorities being apparently unable to cope with the situation. There was justification for Mr. Cleveland's action. The conditions in Paint Creek, W. Va., in the spring of 1913 were by no means analogous. There was trouble between the coal miners and the mine owners, but no Federal function suffered violation or interference. However, in order to find an excuse for conducting a Federal inquiry into a State condition, the Senate Committee on Education and Labor was solemnly directed to proceed to Paint Creek and discover "whether or not postal services have been or are being interfered with or obstructed in said coal fields"; and "whether or not the immigration laws of this country have been or are being violated, and whether there were any agreements or combinations entered into contrary to the laws of the United States; and, finally, if any or all of these conditions exist, to investigate and report upon the causes leading to such conditions." Altogether unavailing was the assertion of the Senators from West Virginia that the State authorities were competently handling the situation. Equally futile was the charge that the resolution of authorization offered only a thinly-clad excuse for an unwarranted Federal interference. The resolution was adopted and the Federal committee started upon its mission of inquiry. Its report was not submitted for a year. In the meantime, the strike had been settled; but the upholders of the doctrine of Federal control cited the presence of the Federal committee in the strike region as a powerful factor in restoring peace and order.

The basis of the inquiry into the strike situations in the copper district of Michigan and the coal fields of Colorado was identical with that set forth in the Paint Creek resolution; and the House of Representatives having ordered the investigations, the Congressional Committees visited the respective localities, not hesitating to summon local and State officials and question them as to the reason for the existing conditions. As a result of the inquiry, the request has been made that strikebreakers be barred from going from one State to another, which is a new application of the authority to regulate commerce. There may be some question as to the propriety of Federal invasion of State territory when there is not even *prima facie* evidence that any detail of Federal administration is involved; but there is no disputing the fact that the invaders went armed with a mandate from all the people, issued through their representatives.

It must be admitted, therefore, that the Federal investigators neither violated nor usurped power. They acted in accordance with law, enacted by those to whom the authority to make laws had been duly delegated by the people.

The fight over the so-called Child Labor Law was lengthy and bitterly contested. The opposition to its enactment came mainly from the Southern States, for two reasons—first, because it is in the South that the doctrine of States' rights is finding its last citadel, and, second, because in that section child labor is very largely used. The doctrine of paramount necessity, however, again prevailed and the measure became a law. In this case, as in many others, the desired result was attempted to be accomplished through indirection. It was manifestly futile to enact a law which should directly supplant the legislation of a State, but it was apparently possible to forbid the interstate shipment of any product of a mine or quarry upon which a child under sixteen years of age had labored or the product of any mill, cannery, workshop, factory or manufacturing establishment whereon children under the age of fourteen years, or children between the ages of fourteen and sixteen years, had labored, except that in the latter case employment during eight hours between six o'clock a. m., and seven o'clock p. m., was permitted. This prohibition accomplished, of course, the reform so imperatively demanded by existing conditions; and although the Supreme Court of the United States, by the narrow majority of five to four, has declared the law unconstitutional, there is no doubt that Congress will amend the act so as to overcome this adverse decision. The reasons which have compelled the enactment of beneficent and humane Federal laws obtain with especial force in the matter of child labor and eventually the proposed and necessary reform will be secured.

Another wide application of Federal power is embodied in the Federal Farm Loan Act, which was approved July 17, 1916. This law was inspired by the fact that while bank loans could be obtained upon stocks and bonds of approved security, the farmer was financially handicapped because he owned nothing but his land. It is not necessary here to review the four years of agitation which preceded the enactment of the law nor to rehearse the obvious arguments which were advanced by those who favored the legislation. Suffice it to say that, it being apparently taken for granted that the States have neither the desire nor the ability to provide for the financial needs of the farmers within their borders, there is now a Federal Farm Loan Board, consisting of five members, including the Secretary of the Treasury, who is chairman *ex-officio*. This Board has divided the United States into twelve districts and has established Federal land banks, each with a subscribed capital of not less than $750,000. National farm loan associations have also been organized under the provisions of the act, and, in fact, thousands of needy farmers have already been accommodated with funds. In view of the certainty that the operations of these Federal banks will extend into every community it is quite evident that the country will now witness in widespread fashion another demonstration of the beneficence of Federal power when exercised for the general good. It is really not a far cry from these Federal farm loan banks to the governmental pawnshops maintained for the poor by France and Mexico. If for the stockholder and bondholder the government can provide a method of borrowing, and if the same advantage can be accorded the owner of land, there is no reason why equal consideration should not be given to the citizen who can only pledge his personal effects. The whole transaction is merely one of degree.

The bold stroke by which Congress established eight hours as a day's work on every railroad in the United States, except those less than 100 miles in length or street or interurban roads operated by electricity, is another extension of Federal power not to be lightly considered. The importance of the enactment is not alone in the fact that Congress can, almost over-night, effect an industrial revolution, but in its demonstration that we too often do our national thinking in terms of politics—a lesson which is serious enough if we are to continue moving forward along present lines. The demand of the 2,000,000 employees, known in railroad circles as the Four Brotherhoods, for the legal establishment of an eight-hour day, was coupled with the threat of a nation-wide strike and that, too, with a presidential election only sixty days distant. It was manifestly fatal for the Administration in power, from a political point of view, either for the strike to occur or for the Brotherhoods to fail in their desire. Consequently the law was hastily framed and passed with equal precipitancy, being approved by the President on September 3, 1916. The oft-repeated experiment of utilizing interstate commerce as the agency to make the law effective was resorted to, as it can be at any time in the future when the organized employees of the railroads decide to formulate additional demands, especially as the Supreme Court of the United States has decided that in the Constitutional right to "regulate commerce" is embraced the authority to specify hours of labor. Nor is it necessary to confine the outlook to railroad employees alone. Any class of men, sufficiently numerous and well-organized, can secure the same result. If a demagogue should reach the White House and truckle for votes in order to secure his reëlection, and if a Congress of cowardly politicians should appear equally desirous of catering to those upon whom their retention in office largely depends, we might easily be confronted with a menacing situation.

The path which has been opened by the passage of the eight-hour law is a wide one and no one can tell whither it will lead. Not so long ago some of the States enacted what are known as "full-crew" railroad laws but in other States similar measures were defeated. There is nothing to prevent a Federal law being enacted which will fasten the desired legislation upon all the States. All social and industrial reforms may be accomplished in the same manner. Woman suffrage, with women wielding the ballot in more than twenty States, must be seriously regarded. When the women voters desire to invoke Federal power in behalf of altruistic principles and back their appeal with promise of support or threat of antagonism at the polls, the laws which they propose will be enacted, and the units which we now designate by the name of States may find themselves more atrophied than ever.

Perhaps, after all, the climax of Federalism is to be found in the so-called Federal Reserve Act. Under this law, which has reformed the currency system of the country, a Federal Reserve Board has been appointed. It consists of seven members of whom two are the Secretary of the Treasury and the Comptroller of the Currency. The other five are named by the President and confirmed by the Senate. As all the national banks are required by the law to enter the Federal Reserve system or forfeit their charters, with the privilege of similar affiliation accorded to State banks and trust companies, the entire monetary system of the country is thus placed under supervision of seven men, all of whom are, in turn, appointees, and to that extent creatures, of the President. The total capitalization of the 7,579 national banks thus brought together is over $1,000,000,000. Their deposits reach the tremendous aggregate of $22,882,000,000 additional and this amount will be enormously increased by the receipts of the government, which are now deposited in the reserve banks instead of the Federal Treasury. Here, then, are seven men, located in the National Capital, agents of the Federal government, virtually holding many billions of dollars. While the wisdom of legalizing this enormous power seems now unquestioned, it is appropriate to recall the memorable fight made by Andrew Jackson against the Bank of the United States. There is a difference, of course, between that institution and the Federal Reserve banks controlled by the Federal Reserve Board, because the former was a private concern, even though chartered by Congress, while the latter are directly under government control.

At the same time, the words of Andrew Jackson are not altogether without bearing upon the present situation. His struggle against the Bank was based upon his antagonism to the control of a vast amount of wealth by a certain few; yet the Bank of the United States dealt with millions where the Federal Reserve Board has to do with billions. The Bank of the United States, as Jackson pointed out, "possessed the power to make money plentiful or scarce at its pleasure at any time or at any place by controlling the issues of other banks and permitting an expansion or compelling a general contraction of the circulating medium according to its will." This criticism applies with equal force to the Federal Reserve Board. It was also Jackson's opinion that "to give the President the control over the currency and the power over individuals now possessed by the Bank of the United States, even with the material difference that he is responsible to the people, would be as objectionable and dangerous as to leave it where it is." It is not a far cry from this declaration of Jackson to the system now enacted into law; and a feeling of anxiety naturally arises at the thought that some day there may be in the White House a President who would convert the Federal Reserve Board into an instrument for the accomplishment of his revenge or the furtherance of his ambition. Upon these seven men there rests a great responsibility. They can use the Federal power, as no other men can, to press the sensitive money nerve of the nation; and yet it must again be emphasized that this power was granted by the representatives of the people. It is true that the legislation which authorized it was recommended and urged with much insistence by the President, but it was not incumbent upon Congress to unwillingly heed the presidential demand. Whether the control of billions of dollars by Federal agents is to be for good or ill, the representatives of the people are responsible and the people themselves must accept the consequences.

As an evidence that we have not reached the limit of the application of Federal power, shoals of measures are introduced in each succeeding session of Congress pointing the way to further extensions. For instance, Maryland, Rhode Island, New York, New Jersey, and West Virginia having adopted State laws to eliminate idleness, and these laws having been executed with some degree of success, it is now proposed, through Federal legislation, to apply the same idea to the entire nation. There are also propositions to punish the false advertisement of any security or commodity which enters into interstate commerce; to establish uniform prices for uniform commodities; to attach a

Federal label to all fabrics and leather goods; to provide for the Federal inspection and grading of grain; and to fix the size of fruit baskets. The National Wage Commission bill has many advocates. It provides that the President shall appoint a wage commissioner for each Congressional district in the United States to investigate every complaint of alleged insufficient, inequitable or unjust wage. This, of course, would be Federal interference, supervision and control to the last degree. Senator Chilton, of Texas, has seriously proposed that the Federal Government shall establish a minimum wage of $9 per week for all females employed by persons, firms or corporations doing an interstate commerce business. Another proposition defines and regulates investment companies authorized to use the mail and makes the very act of using the mails a sufficient foundation for bringing any person, firm or corporation within the sphere of Federal control.

These instances could be multiplied. They illustrate the tendency of the times. There is absolutely no limit to the phases which invite the application of Federal authority, apart from any question of war emergency. Congress has already gone far; but judging the future from the past, it has only touched the edges of the great domain wherein Federal power may be exerted. No one can examine the record of the laws already passed, nor scan the list of measures awaiting action, without realizing that popular approval is bestowed upon every effort to invoke Federal aid in the securement of beneficent results.

Chapter IX

THE SUPREME COURT AS THE BULWARK OF FEDERALISM

THE people, through their representatives, invoked Federal aid to remedy nation-wide evils and prevent monopolistic domination. Those upon whom the heavy hand of Federal power was laid have appealed, in turn, to the Supreme Court of the United States. They have raised grave questions of constitutional interpretation and upon the decision of these questions much has depended. Fortunately for the people, the Supreme Court has approached the legal problems presented for its adjudication with a high conception of the responsibilities involved. More than this, it apparently has realized that only through the employment of the methods which the people had devised could the much-desired reforms be accomplished. It has, therefore, persistently upheld all forms of Congressional legislation. It has been the very bulwark of Federalism. It has gone to the utmost limit in affording a judicial foundation for Federal control.

It is well that this has been the case. If instead of being in thorough sympathy with the spirit which created the Interstate Commerce Commission and which inspired the Anti-Lottery Law, the Anti-Trust Law, the Pure Food Law, the White Slave Law, and the scores of other Federal enactments which entrusted Federal agents with the protection of life, health and morals of the people, the Supreme Court had displayed an antagonistic sentiment, the accomplishment of reform would have been delayed. It would not have been prevented, for, sooner or later, the people would have found some way to reach the desired end. The movement to resolve all questions of constitutional construction at the ballot box or the attempt to secure easy and frequent amendment of the Constitution, would have been greatly stimulated and, finally, prevailed. The fact is, however, that the Supreme Court, although its members are properly far removed from political influence and popular clamor, has been thoroughly cognizant of and responsive to the increasing demand for the betterment of human life and its environment. No one to-day asks, with the guilty evasion of Cain, "Am I my brother's keeper?" On the contrary, the responsibility of brotherhood is universally avowed and accepted. Legislation tainted with a suspicion of sordidness and selfishness, which benefits the few at the expense of the many, is shunned as an evil thing, while propositions that seek to ameliorate human conditions are stamped with legislative approval.

With this spirit the Supreme Court is in entire harmony. A statement recently made public shows that out of 563 decisions rendered between 1887 and 1911 upon questions involving what are known as social justice laws, it has rendered affirmative opinions in all but three. One of these held invalid an anti-trust law of Illinois because it illegally discriminated in favor of certain classes. The second nullified a statute of Louisiana which forbade citizens to order insurance through the mail from foreign insurance companies, it being held that this law was an interference with the liberty of contract. The third was the famous bakeshop case, in which the court held unconstitutional the bakers' ten-hour day law in New York. On the other hand, it has sustained State laws for the suppression of gambling and bucket-shop and option speculation, for the prohibition of the sale of liquor and cigarettes, for the regulation of corporations, the safety of miners and the abolition of child labor, and numerous other equally commendable objects. It has allied itself with the modern prohibition movement so thoroughly as to declare that the right to sell intoxicating liquors is not one of the privileges and immunities of citizenship granted by the Constitution. It has compelled the deportation of alien prostitutes and not only has it decided the White Slave Act to be constitutional, but has upheld it in every case, both in letter and spirit, even to the extent of declaring that it does not impinge upon the reserved police powers of the State. With this knowledge of the high ideals which actuate the minds of the members of the Supreme Court, it is easy to appreciate its friendly attitude toward Federal legislation which seeks the betterment of the entire people.

It might be supposed that the Supreme Court, in thus sustaining State progressive legislation, is committed to the idea that through the States, rather than through Federal agency, the largest degree of accomplishment is possible. Such, however, is not the case. It aids and abets the States in their praiseworthy endeavors until Federal laws are enacted and then it instantly recognizes the supremacy of Congressional action. Being observant, it is fully aware that the enactments of State legislatures are necessarily restricted in their beneficial effect. Each State is only one-forty-eighth of the whole. The State may do certain things, as was held in one of the Employers' Liability cases, until Congress exercises its constitutional function, and then the Federal legislation supersedes all State law upon that subject. Realizing that a Federal law benefits the entire nation, the court, whenever such is brought to its attention, hastens to sustain its legality if it rests upon the slightest foundation of constitutional authority. There have been only a few adverse rulings. One was the decision against the income tax law, the unconstitutionality of which was narrowly affirmed by a vote of five to four. The people have since remedied this defeat of their expressed will by adding an amendment to the Constitution. Another was the decision in which the first Employers' Liability Act was held to be invalid because it included within its provisions an employee not engaged in interstate commerce. Congress thereupon passed an amended measure which has not only been sustained but has been declared to be paramount to all State laws.

The restraining hand of Federal power has been laid by the Supreme Court upon State legislatures which sought to bargain away the public health and the public morals, while peonage, allowed under the laws and decisions of some States, has been declared to be involuntary servitude within the meaning of the Constitution. The limitation upon State action is fully set forth in the decision in the case of Taylor *vs.* Thomas, in which it is declared that judicial and legislative acts of a State, hostile in their purpose or mode of enforcement to the authority of the Federal Government, or which impair the rights of citizens under the Federal Constitution, are invalid and void. In the enforcement of the Fourteenth amendment, which provides that "no State shall make or enforce any law which shall abridge the privileges or immunities of citizens of the United States; nor shall any State deprive any person of life, liberty or property, without due process of the law; nor deny to any person within its jurisdiction the equal protection of its laws," the Supreme Court has demanded of the States a strict accountability.

Numerous decisions have been rendered which

insist that the prohibitions of this amendment extend to all the acts of a State, whether exercised through its legislative, its executive or its judicial authorities. The Court has even gone beyond the text of a State law to determine whether an unjust purpose was concealed. Take, for instance, the ordinance of the San Francisco supervisors which provided that no laundry should be operated except in a building constructed of brick or stone. This was plainly discriminatory legislation. The Supreme Court decided that "though a law be fair upon its face and impartial in its appearance, yet if it is administered by public authority with an evil eye and an unequal hand so as to make illegal discrimination between persons in similar circumstances," it violates the Constitution by being a denial of equal rights. Hundreds of cases of real or fancied partiality on the part of a State for one citizen as against another have been patiently heard by the Supreme Court, including even the question whether osteopaths in Texas are persons practicing medicine, and where injustice has been proven, the Federal power has been interposed and equity secured. There would be no necessity for these appeals if the States did not occasionally stray from the path of even-handed justice and grant favors to their own citizens which they are unwilling to accord to others. Tennessee, for instance, enacted a statute which gave to residents of the State priority over nonresidents in the distribution of the assets of a foreign corporation. The Supreme Court declared that these selfish privileges could not be granted and through the exercise of the Federal power prevented the consummation of an evident wrong. It declared invalid the Oklahoma law which forbade foreign corporations from appealing to the Federal Courts and held unconstitutional the South Dakota statute making railroad corporations liable for double damages in certain cases. More than this, the Supreme Court has jealously guarded the constitutional powers of Congress as to the right to regulate commerce and has prevented any encroachment upon these powers by the States.

A natural corollary of the Court's position in maintaining Federal supremacy over the States has been the upholding of Federal legislation. The principle prevails that Congress must violently disregard a plain provision of the Constitution before the Supreme Court will undertake to set aside the will of the people as expressed through their representatives. Once in a while this happens, and when Congress passed a law declaring it a criminal offense for any agent or officer of an interstate carrier to discharge an employee of that carrier because of his membership in a labor organization, the Court held that the statute was an invasion of personal liberty and the rights of property. At the same time, these adverse decisions are the exceptions rather than the rule. On the other hand, it has held that the constitutional guarantee of religious freedom was not intended to prohibit legislation against polygamy. When it was claimed that the Federal power could not keep lottery advertisements out of the newspapers because such restriction abridged the liberty of the press, the Court decided that the law was valid. The constitutionality of the Legal Tender Acts was sustained as being the proper means of carrying into execution the legitimate powers of the government.

The Court's belief in the power of the Federal government over corporations is shown in the numerous decisions sustaining the Sherman Anti-Trust Law. Notwithstanding the fact that it read the word "reasonable" into the statute, it has dissolved the Sugar Trust, the Standard Oil Trust, the Tobacco Trust, and other gigantic combinations. It over-ruled the consolidation of the Northern Pacific and Great Northern railroads, known as the Northern Securities Company, and compelled the Union Pacific railroad to surrender the stock of the Southern Pacific railroad which it had acquired. In at least four important cases, including the famous litigation against the Danbury Hatters' Union, it interposed the Federal power against aggrieved labor organizations. In the Trans-Missouri Freight Association case it applied the Sherman Law to railroad corporations in order to protect the people; and in all of the other cases which have engaged its attention it over-ruled contentions which shrewd lawyers brought forward to prevent the law from being operative against conspiracies in restraint of trade. In the same broad manner it has dealt with the law to regulate commerce, under which the Interstate Commerce Commission was created, and has made the railroads subservient to Federal authority. It has sustained that Commission whenever possible. It has even gone so far as to decide, in the Chicago Junction railway case, that service performed entirely within a State is still subject to the provisions of Federal legislation if it is a part of interstate commerce, and has declared that since the passage of the Hepburn Act it is beyond the power of a State to regulate even the delivery of cars for interstate shipments. It has prevented the courts from setting aside, under the guise of exerting judicial power, certain orders of the Interstate Commerce Commission, and has sustained the Act which forbids interstate carriers from transporting articles or commodities in which they had a legal ownership. It sustained the Hours of Service Act upon the ground that each over-worked employee presents toward the public a distinct source of danger. Its decision upholding the law against railroad rebates abolished that evil for all time, while the verdict of legality which it gave to the corporation income tax law of 1913 enabled the government instantly to add $30,000,000 annually to the Federal treasury.

Not only has the Supreme Court thus given the force of judicial sanction to Federal laws which increase Federal power but it has, in more cases than one, opened wide the door of refuge in a Federal court. It has declared, in the case of the Union Pacific Railroad *vs.* Myers, that "it is sufficient for the jurisdiction of the United States if the suit involves necessarily a question depending upon the Constitution, laws and treaties of the United States." In another case it is asserted that the fact that a party to an action is a corporation created by the laws of the United States makes the question a Federal one for the purpose of jurisdiction by a circuit court. Still further, in the case of Nashville *vs.* Cooper, it was held that "it is no objection to the jurisdiction of the Federal courts that questions are involved which are not all of a Federal character. If one of the latter exists," it was added, "the court, having assumed jurisdiction, will proceed to decide every question in the case." Having expressed these and kindred views, it is easy to understand how the Supreme Court promptly brushed aside the contention that the Federal laws which authorized Federal officials to make rules and regulations were unconstitutional in that they invested the executive branch of the government with legislative or judicial functions. This was the argument made against the orders of the Interstate Commerce Commission; against the regulations prescribed by the Commissioner of Internal Revenue in connection with the marks and brands upon packages of oleomargarine; against the power delegated to the Secretary of the Treasury to establish standards of tea; against the authority given to the Secretary of War to determine whether a bridge is an unreasonable obstruction to navigation; against the power lodged with the Secretary of Agriculture making criminal all violations of the rules and regulations promulgated by him for the control of forest reservations; and, most important of all, when it was claimed to be an absolutely unwarranted delegation of legislative power to the Federal executive to authorize the President, in the Tariff Act of October 1, 1890, to suspend upon a given contingency the provisions of an act relating to the free importation of certain articles.

All of these contentions the Supreme Court over-ruled, asserting that Congress may, in its discretion, employ any appropriate means not forbidden by the Constitution to carry into effect and accomplish the objects of a power given to it by the Constitution. In other words, it is now a well-established principle that if Congress seeks to attain certain necessary results, the employment of delegated power to secure those results is perfectly justifiable. If the Court had held otherwise the work of the Federal legislature would have been tedious and intricate. As it is, upon the strength of these decisions, it is only necessary for Congress to determine, on behalf of the people, that certain things must be done and then authorize some Federal agent to devise the details by which the law can be made effective. It must be admitted, however, that the line of demarcation between the legislative and the executive function almost disappears when comprehensive rules and regulations, which have the force of law, are promulgated by the official head of a Federal department.

It must not be understood, however, that the Supreme Court in thus vitalizing Federal control, has entirely disregarded the State as an entity. In the Minnesota and Missouri railroad rate cases it admitted the right of a State railroad commission to fix maximum intrastate rates, although it reserved the authority to determine whether these rates were reasonable or confiscatory. It has uniformly held that the first clause of the seventh amendment to the Constitution in regard to the right of trial by jury relates only to Federal courts and that the States are left to regulate trials in their own courts. It regards the first ten amendments to the Constitution as being limitations exclusively upon Federal power. It also admits that "the State has undoubtedly the power by appropriate legislation to protect the public morals, the public health and the public safety," the only restriction being that it must afford every person the equal protection of its laws. It also leaves to State constitutions and State laws the protection of property from unjust or oppressive local taxation. Regarding the recognition of the police powers of the State, it has held that these powers may be exercised when they "do not interfere with the powers or Constitution of the General Government." The intimation of reserved Federal powers in all the decisions relating to the police powers of the States is significant. Already, in the settlement of social problems, Federal laws are trenching closely upon the police powers of the State; and in the near future, when these enactments are brought before the Supreme Court, that tribunal will felicitate itself upon the foresight which led it to suggest that even upon the police powers of the State there are constitutional limitations.

It is impossible, within the compass of a single chapter, to more fully discuss the Federalistic trend of the decisions of the Supreme Court. Enough has been given, however, to demonstrate that the members of that great tribunal are thoroughly imbued with the wisdom and importance of strengthening the arm of the Federal government. Adopting the theory of Marshall that the Constitution was ordained and established by the people of the United States for themselves, for their own government, and not for the government of the individual States, they have found in that Constitution ample justification for every step which the people have taken toward investing the Federal government with additional power.

Chapter X

THE POWER OF THE PRESIDENT

THE growth of the Federal power has been due to the representatives of the people. The embodiment of that power is the President of the United States. This could not be otherwise. Power is ineffective unless exercised through executive agency; and so, more and more, the authority which has been conferred upon the Federal Government has carried with it an increase of power for the head of that government.

It must be borne in mind that no President can escape the atmosphere of Federalism with which he is surrounded. His position compels a nation-wide point of view. Senators and Representatives, no matter how broad-minded and patriotic they may be, are likely to be concerned with matters that virtually affect their especial States or districts. The President, on the other hand, being responsible for the destiny of the nation as a whole, and being dependent politically upon the commendation of all the people, cannot limit the sphere of his activities to the narrow confines of a State. Every President has, by the very circumstance of his position, become an upholder of the doctrine of Federalism. Even Thomas Jefferson became nationalized, so to speak, after his election to the presidency. In recent years an immense amount of responsibility has been placed upon the President; and, more than once, Presidents have used the prestige and power of their position to accomplish the enactment into law of policies which they personally deemed of benefit to the people of the United States.

Examples of this character have been especially frequent during the last two decades. When, for instance, President Cleveland came into power on March 4, 1893, he found upon the statute books a law authorizing the purchase of 4,500,000 ounces of silver each month. Whether the operation of this act was responsible for the financial troubles then beginning to affect the country was, in the public mind, still an open question; but in the judgment of the President there was no doubt whatever. In the message submitted by him to Congress at the beginning of the special session which he convened, he laid all the blame at the door of the statute and demanded its repeal. He did not confine his effort to the constitutional limitation of communicating his views to Congress, but brought personal pressure to bear upon the legislative branch of the government. Even now one can recall how the emissaries of the President thronged the corridors of the capitol; how strange and remarkable conversions were wrought through influences which emanated from the White House and which it was not politic to withstand. When the bill repealing the silver-purchasing law went to the Senate it did not command a majority of that body; but during the ensuing three months of acrimonious debate, the power of the President was exerted to such an extent as to win to the support of the measure the votes needed to overcome the deficiency. No one who is at all familiar with the inner history of that memorable and most dramatic struggle will dispute these statements.

In the McKinley administration the power of the President turned the wavering scale in favor of the ratification of the treaty of peace with Spain, wherein it was proposed to pay $20,000,000 for the acquisition of the Philippines, although that territory had already been obtained through conquest. President Roosevelt successfully exerted tremendous pressure upon Congress to secure the enactment of the law widely extending the powers of the Interstate Commerce Commission, the Porto Rican tariff law and many other measures. Nothing less than the power of the President could have secured the passage, during President Taft's administration, of the law concerning reciprocity with Canada. And since President Wilson has been in the White House there has been a constant exhibition of the power of the President over Congress. In the preparation of the tariff bill he demanded that his own views be followed, not only as to the principles but as to the very details of the proposed law. When he insisted that it was necessary to enact a law reforming the currency system, Congress remained in Washington during the long, hot summer months, in obedience to his will, while the spectacle was afforded of Senators and Representatives being summoned to the White House, to receive, even at midnight conferences, the executive direction. Another striking instance was the enactment of the law repealing the exemption of American coastwise vessels from the payment of Panama canal tolls. In the face of well-founded opposition, President Wilson demanded of Congress that the repeal should be effected, and Congress obeyed. There has hardly been an instance during the past twenty years wherein any President has been defeated in any effort vigorously prosecuted by him to secure the enactment of legislation upon which he had deliberately determined.

It is not difficult to discover the source of the executive power. It lies very largely in the distribution of patronage. A golden stream flows through the White House to the remotest corner of the country. It springs from the national treasury. Under present conditions, any President of the United States has the power to divert this stream where and whither he will—into the pockets, occasionally, of his personal friends, but invariably to the financial benefit of his political supporters. If money is the lever that rules the world any President can dispense it with a largess that is startling. He can stand beside the public treasury, with one arm plunged deep into its vaults, while the other distributes the golden store to a horde of office-holders. Postmasters, collectors of customs, revenue officials, marshals, attorneys, consuls, foreign ministers—all these and more are recipients of bounty through presidential favor. The only check is the approval of the United States Senate on appointments; and the members of that body, knowing that their constituents are drinking deeply of the Pactolian stream, rarely interpose an objection. Ten years ago official figures obtained from the Government departments, not including the War and Navy Departments, showed that the President directly controlled appointments which paid salaries amounting to approximately $20,000,000 a year. Since that time the number of Federal offices has been so greatly increased, as a natural accompaniment of the growth of Federal power, that the total is now appalling in its magnitude. Statistics compiled by the Civil Service Commission show that on June 30, 1917, the number of officers and employees in the Federal civil service was 517,805. Excluding employees who are within the scope of competitive examination, or who are laborers engaged in Panama Canal work and elsewhere, as well as mail contractors, there were, on the date mentioned, 125,129 persons who came within the presidential power of appointment or were directly or indirectly named by heads of departments selected by the President. The annual salaries paid to these appointed employees would certainly aggregate a quarter of a billion dollars. The spoils of office which figured so largely in Andrew Jackson's administration were as a tiny rivulet compared with the mighty patronage of a President at the present time. The hand which controls this enormous output of national wealth is a hand of power.

Presidential pressure upon Congress is tolerated upon the theory that the end justifies the means, because in practically every instance where legislation has been forced through Congress the President was apparently actuated by sincere motives. The argument is not sound. If the presidential power can be exercised for good it may also be made an agency for evil. The fact is that it ought not to be exerted at all. Under the Constitution the Government is divided into three branches, the legislative, executive and judicial. They are distinct and separate in their functions and in their relations to each other. It never was intended that the executive should trench upon the legislative, other than through the occasional presentation of a message upon the state of the nation. It is one of the evils of the growth of Federal power that the President has been afforded an opportunity for conferring favors upon Senators and Representatives in the matter of appointments to a degree which makes the situation serious.

With the knowledge that the attitude of an administration toward his candidacy may make him or break him, few legislators dare to be *persona non grata* with a President of their political faith. Their sphere of usefulness in the preparation of laws may not be interfered with, but they are politically weakened if they are deprived of presidential recognition and support. Perhaps we shall some day have a law which will forbid presidential influence in elections. In the meantime, the politicians will continue to follow the line of least resistance; and it is always easier for them to plead party regularity and justify adherence to a President than it is to explain opposition. Senators and Representatives also align themselves with an administration of their own party because they know that if the President is sustained by the country, their own retention in office is more certainly assured; while if the President is repudiated, they will go down with their party, no matter whether they were with the President or against him. When it comes to dealing with the people, however, the presidential power is not always effective. The power of patronage renominated President Harrison in 1892 and President Taft in 1912, but both were defeated at the polls. It is a reassuring fact that no President has yet been able to build up an office-holding oligarchy that will absolutely insure his reëlection; but it is also a fact that through the distribution of Federal patronage an influence can be exerted over Congress which, in the hands of an unscrupulous man, might become a menace to the country.

There is another reason why the power of the President has so greatly increased. Congress is apparently quite willing to place the burden of government upon his shoulders. This was evident before the outbreak of the war; and since war has been declared nearly every legislative act of importance has added to the President's duties and responsibilities. Some of these measures have been of the President's own seeking; but all of them have added so tremendously to his authority that he is to-day invested with more power than any other ruler in the world. In the food and fuel administration bill, for instance, he is given practically absolute control over the transportation and distribution of food-stuffs; the power to fix prices; to fix the standards and grades of foodstuffs; to commandeer supplies and even take over plants, either for the armed forces or for the public good; to license the importation, exportation, manufacture, storage and distribution of the necessaries of life; to prevent waste and hoarding; to purchase, store and sell necessaries at reasonable prices; and to prohibit the use of foods, fruits, food materials or feeds in the production of distilled liquors, except for governmental, industrial or medicinal purposes. He has been given the power to commandeer ships and ship-construction plants; to declare embargoes; to determine priority of shipments of commodities by any common carriers; to affect our international relations and the conduct of the war by loaning $3,000,000,000 to our Allies in such manner as his judgment may dictate; to control absolutely the production of aeroplanes, even to the extent of securing land and buildings by any means he sees fit to use; and, omitting a thousand and one other investments of authority, to determine who shall and who shall not be exempted from the operation of the Conscription Law. Is it any wonder that with so much delegated power he should object, as he did in his letter to Representative A. F. Lever, of South Carolina, on July 23, 1917, to the creation of a Committee of Congressional Control on the ground that such supervision would render practically impossible "my task of conducting the war"?

We can accept with more or less equanimity, on account of war conditions, the announcement in the *New York Times,* on the eve of the assembling of the second session of the Sixty-fifth Congress, that "not in years has there been a session of Congress in which the legislative activity depended so entirely upon the initiative of the Executive" and that "leaders on both sides of the capitol say that they will be guided in their legislative work by the wishes of the President." The Washington correspondent of the *New York World* asserted on Monday, December 3, 1917, that Congress would "leave everything to 'The Man in the White House,' " and added that "his authority is absolute, his wish equal to a command." It is not a healthy symptom when we, as a people, are urged to "stand by the President," as if the other branches of our tripartite government were of no concern whatever . This reminds one of the English motto, "For God, for King, for Country," the ruler being placed ahead of the nation. The time is coming, however, when the war will be over, and when the President cannot have the excuse of abnormal conditions for exercising an unprecedented degree of autocratic power. Judging the future by the past, we will find that no President will willingly surrender any degree of authority which he has enjoyed. None the less must we face squarely the constantly enlarging executive power.

One method of divorcing the executive from the distribution of patronage was presented in a speech delivered in the United States Senate some years ago by Senator Jonathan Bourne, Jr., of Oregon, who proposed a constitutional amendment transferring the presidential power of nomination to a permanent non-partisan commission to be created, with the suggestion that, in the meantime, the responsibility for selection should be placed upon Senators and Representatives. Mr. Bourne expressed the hope that the crystallization of public opinion against the misuse of power by the President would force presidential candidates in all parties to announce, prior to their nomination or election, that if elected they would place upon Senators and Representatives the responsibility for making selections of all Federal appointees in their respective States. Experience has demonstrated, however, that these suggestions are neither wise nor practical. The plan of a nonpartisan commission to make appointments was unsuccessfully experimented with in New York State from 1780 to 1820. The investment of Senators and Representatives with the power of selection would result in a diffused responsibility which would plague the country. Legislative designation has been tried and abandoned in nearly all the States in which appointments by the legislature once obtained.

Even if there unfortunately should be a disposition to place upon national legislators the responsibility of naming Federal office-holders, we are confronted by the fact that neither Presidents nor would-be Presidents will relinquish, or promise to relinquish, the machinery of control which now exists in the distribution of patronage. That they should be willing to do so is true enough; but what they ought to do and what they will agree to do, are two very different propositions. They will continue to use the power of patronage to influence those who are disposed to be recalcitrant; not always, of course, in the unconcealed fashion of President Taft. There is nothing more remarkable in the whole realm of political correspondence than the letter which was made public on September 15, 1910, and signed by Charles D. Norton, then Secretary to President Taft. This communication, addressed to a Republican party leader in Iowa whose name was not disclosed, frankly stated that "while certain legislation pending in Congress was opposed by certain Republicans, the President felt it to be his duty to his party and to the country to withhold Federal patronage from certain Senators and Congressmen who seemed to be in opposition to the administration's efforts to carry out the promises of the party platform." Here, then, was a direct admission that the President had so manipulated the distribution of Federal offices as to punish those who were not in accord with his policies; and although it was added that this discrimination had ceased, the fact that it had been practiced was unblushingly confessed. Other Presidents, with more political shrewdness and less innate honesty than President Taft, have never yet taken the people into their confidence to the same extent, although it is no matter of doubt that they have been equally reprehensible.

The power of the President to shape national policies is not confined to his control over Congress. Five of the nine Associate Justices now serving upon the bench of the Supreme Court of the United States were appointed by President Taft, who also nominated the present Chief Justice; and it is safe to say that Mr. Taft was thoroughly conversant with the views held by each appointee upon constitutional and other questions before he submitted their names to the Senate, and that each of them reflected his own opinions. The same assertion applies to the appointment of Mr. Brandeis and Mr. Clark by President Wilson. The policy of the government toward the railroads was also affected in the past by the personnel of the Interstate Commerce Commission. Recently there was a prolonged contest over the confirmation of an appointee to this Commission, on the ground that his acts and utterances betrayed too plainly his attitude toward the railroads; but the President insisted upon favorable action and was victorious. The President can also put men in his cabinet as the first step toward effecting policies which do not require legislative sanction, but which may materially affect the nation or the perpetuation of his party in power. There are, in fact, so many ways in which the power of the President can be and is exercised, apart from insisting that Congress shall do his will, that unless that power is safeguarded more carefully than at present, the door of danger is opened wide.

Chapter XI

FEDERAL POWER AS A POLITICAL ISSUE

THE political system which has developed in the United States is one of party government. It is important, therefore, that each party should clearly and carefully define its position in order that the people may be able to decide intelligently which organization to support by their votes. There have been innumerable issues since the election of our first President, but none presents a more interesting subject for study and analysis than the question of the limitation and extent of Federal power. This is especially true of the early days of the Republic when the acceptance of Federal power was not as universal as it is to-day.

It is a significant fact that the first words of the first platform adopted by the Democratic party set forth a principle to which that party clung tenaciously for many years. "Resolved," said this declaration, "that the Federal government is one of limited powers." This was in 1840. For nearly half a century the Democrats had been in power. Jefferson, Madison, Monroe, Jackson and Van Buren had been elected, and even though the term of John Quincy Adams intervened, the fact is that he received a much smaller popular vote than Jackson and became President only because the election was thrown into the House of Representatives. All these men had been upholders of the rights of the States and were strict constructionists of the Constitution and it was but natural that when it became necessary to present party principles in concrete form the ideas which had led to Democratic success should be definitely expressed. We find, therefore, that not only was it resolved that the Federal government was one of limited powers but that the platform fairly bristled with a series of constitutional "don'ts" designed to restrict the operations of the general government. Among other things, it was declared that there could not be, and should not be, a Federal system of internal improvements—a position upon which the party in later years absolutely reversed itself.

With this issue thus emphasized, the party went down to defeat, William Henry Harrison being elected. It is not enough to say that this was not a case of cause and effect nor that Harrison was elected because he was a more popular candidate than Van Buren. The fact is, and it can be proven, that when the Democratic party decided to make an issue before the people on the question of halting the growth of a strong, centralized government, it invited the long period of successive defeats which followed. Of course, it could not act otherwise. Opposition to the continuance of slavery had already become manifest and there was an increasing tendency to insist that human bondage was an evil which the Federal government should exterminate. The slave-holders in the South, the majority of whom were Democrats, and who controlled the political destinies of Senators and Representatives from their widely extended and important section, insisted that slavery was purely a State matter and that each State must be left to solve the problem in its own way. In 1852 the Democratic platform unequivocally asserted that Congress had no right to interfere with slavery. It went even further. It pledged the Democratic party to faithfully abide by and uphold the principles laid down in the Kentucky and Virginia resolutions of 1792 and 1798. These resolutions, as has been previously shown, breathed defiance of State government to national government; and when the Democratic party adopted these principles "as constituting one of the main foundations of its political creed" and "resolved to carry them out in their obvious meaning and import," it again drew a clear line of demarcation which could not be misinterpreted or misunderstood. Its leaders, suffering political strabismus on account of their devotion to slavery, could not see that their position was untenable and even fatal. It was all the more unfortunate for them that their position rested upon a condition repugnant to the American love of freedom. Subsequent events have proved, however, that their doctrine would have gone down to defeat even if it had rested upon some other foundation.

The Republicans were only too willing to fight out the question of national supremacy over the slavery issue. From the very beginning they were the political successors of Hamilton and all the other ultra-Federalists and the struggle was altogether to their liking. Even before the Civil War the Whigs were declaring for an enlargement of Federal power—the construction of internal improvements and the building of a trans-continental railroad through government aid. After the war the Republicans naturally went farther. They declared in 1872 that the United States is a nation and not a league; and twelve years later expressed the same idea more fully in these words: "The people of the United States in their organized capacity, constitute a nation and not an American federacy of states." The Democrats, in the meantime, so thoroughly were they still obsessed with the ante-war doctrines, held to their old position. Even as late as 1880 they were declaring opposition to centralization and to "that dangerous spirit of encroachment which tends to consolidate the powers of all the departments in one and thus to create, whatever be the form of government, a real despotism."

It was not until 1884 that a light broke upon the Democratic vision. The party had long been out of power. Its members had seen the Republicans forging ahead, holding control because they were constantly finding new avenues for the exercise of Federal power, and it seemed to finally dawn upon them that perhaps they had failed to sense accurately the American spirit. In their platform for 1884 a significant sentence occurs.

No longer do they reiterate with futile frequency the idea that the Federal government is one of limited powers. On the contrary, we now learn that "as the nation grows older, new issues are born of time and progress and old issues perish." There is even for the first time an admission of "the supremacy of the Federal government," even though the phrase be qualified with reference to "the reserved rights of the States" and "the limits of the Constitution." A remarkable result followed. The Democratic party, for the first time in a quarter of a century, elected its President. It is far more reasonable to believe that the Democrats were victorious because they frankly confessed the errors of the past and entered upon a path in which nation-loving citizens could join them than to assert that a single remark by a public speaker about rum, Romanism and rebellion occasioned Blaine's defeat.

With a fatuity that seems inexplicable the Democratic party failed to hold the advanced position which it had taken and in 1888 again declared its devotion to a strict construction of the Constitution, with consequent defeat. In 1892 it attempted to carry water on both shoulders. In one paragraph of its platform it deplored that "the tendency to centralize all power at the Federal capital has become a menace to the reserved rights of the States, that strikes at the very roots of our government under the Constitution as framed by the fathers of the Republic." This declaration lost whatever force an obsolete doctrine might have had when it was placed alongside other utterances in the same platform. While decrying centralized power in one breath, the platform almost immediately thereafter favored "legislation by Congress and State legislatures to protect the lives and the limbs of railway employees and those of other hazardous transportation companies." More than this, the platform declared that "the Federal government shall care for and improve the Mississippi river and other great waterways of the Republic, so as to secure for the interior States easy and cheap transportation to tide water. When any waterway of the republic is of sufficient importance to demand the aid of the government," the platform continued, "such aid should be extended with a definite plan of continuous work until permanent improvement is secured." The changes which the years had wrought in the evolution of Federal power are made wonderfully apparent in the paragraph just quoted. The idea that the Federal government was constitutionally helpless to enter within a State boundary, even to conduct a public improvement—an idea emphatically asserted as a party principle in 1840—had in 1892 passed into oblivion. Upon this platform of 1892 the Democrats won.

Once again, in 1896, the Democratic party harked back to its old love and declared that it had "resisted the tendency of selfish interests to the centralization of governmental power and steadfastly maintained the integrity of the dual system of government established by the founders of this republic of republics." There was also a touch of pride in the declaration that "under its guidance and teachings the great principle of local self-government has found its best expression in the maintenance of the rights of the States and in its assertion of the necessity of confining the general government to the exercise of the powers granted by the Constitution of the United States."

On the other hand, the Republican party broadened its growing catalogue of Federal activities and won the election. In the following campaign of 1900 the Democrats, still failing to realize that their fight to limit Federal powers had been a hopeless one, undertook the equally impossible task of minimizing the international power which had been thrust upon the United States as the outcome of the war with Spain. "The burning issue of imperialism, growing out of the Spanish War," declared the platform, "involves the very existence of the Republic and the destruction of our free institutions. We regard it as the paramount issue of the campaign." The issue was repudiated by the people. They were more and more learning and loving national greatness. The process of evolution through which the American people had been advancing for more than a century failed to make its impress upon the Democratic mind and the party went down again to defeat. The fact is that the Democratic party placed a serious handicap upon itself when it declared that the Federal government was one of limited powers. The period between 1860 and 1912 is more than half a century. During all that time the Democrats were in complete possession of both the executive and legislative branches of the government for two years only. Even in 1912 the combined Republican vote was over one million in excess of the Democratic vote. In the election of 1916 the Democrats had so thoroughly begun to invoke and utilize Federal power that the question of dual sovereignty was no longer an issue.

Nothing could better illustrate popular acquiescence in the exercise of the largest possible degree of Federal power than the case of Theodore Roosevelt. When he sought election in 1904, as the successor of the martyred McKinley, the Democratic party indirectly denounced him by favoring "the nomination and election of a President imbued with the principles of the Constitution, who will set his face against executive usurpation of legislative and judicial functions, whether that usurpation be veiled under the guise of executive construction of existing laws or whether it take refuge in the tyrant's plea of necessity or superior wisdom." The denunciation was in vain, even though every one knew that in the matter of Federal control he had gone further than the most daring of his predecessors. It is true that he had expressed his willingness to have the States work out, if they could, the reforms which he regarded as essential to the national welfare, "but," he added significantly, "if the States do not do as they should, there will be no choice but for the National government to interfere." He gave the States their opportunity when he invited the governors to a conference at the White House and listened while they gravely discussed the necessity for uniform legislation along progressive lines. But when the conference did not produce material results, as nobody expected it would, and when the organization then effected subsided into a perfunctory existence, Mr. Roosevelt went ahead and upon his own initiative created various Federal Commissions to inquire into subjects which might properly be considered as belonging exclusively to the jurisdiction of the States. In due course of time he again became a candidate for the Presidency; and although it was evident that he entertained positive ideas of executive power, as shown by his action in the Tennessee Coal and Iron Company case; and although the third-term question entered into his candidacy, over 4,000,000 American citizens cast their votes for him. So thoroughly did he represent the idea that the Federal power should be exerted to the last degree in the effort to ameliorate human conditions that the voters apparently did not care whether he had served two terms or twenty. There is no other reason to account for the very large degree of popular support accorded him except upon the theory that he was the most satisfactory personification of the Federal authority which the people now accepted with implicit faith.

The relation of Federal power to politics is certain to be complicated in the future by the fact that the Federalism of to-day is carrying us steadily toward socialism—not the anarchistic, revolutionary, radical socialism that disregards the inherent rights of property and demands equality at the sacrifice of individuality, but the State socialism which employs the power of the Government to accomplish those desirable and universal results which are not otherwise attainable. The merging of Federalism into Socialism is already apparent. Certain it is that the growth of Federalism—the steadily increasing demand for Federal inspection, regulation and control—has been coincident to and parallel with the spread of the Socialistic sentiment throughout the world. It is State socialism, pure and simple, for the Federal government to investigate causes of infant mortality; to inspect the meats which the people eat and guarantee the purity of the foods and drugs which they buy; to assist the planter in baling his cotton or the farmer in shipping and selling his grain; and to provide employment through the operation of a Federal bureau. Federal legislation to-day is fairly saturated with the germs of Socialism, even though the term is not used, but, sooner or later, the nation will be brought face to face with a demand for laws in which there will be no disguise. If it were not for the fact that the Socialist party, as at present led and constituted, is repellent because of its lack of patriotism and is guilty of arraying class against class, it would have a much larger following than it enjoys. Note, however, that while the Socialists, as a political organization, did not place a Presidential candidate in the field until 1904, they were able to give Eugene V. Debs nearly 1,000,000 votes in 1912. There have been periods during the past five years when more than 1,000 Socialists held elective office in the United States and the number is constantly increasing. In more than one city to-day the Socialists are almost equaling in numbers the voters of the long-established parties and to prevent their further success at the polls it is seriously proposed —and was, in fact, actually practiced recently in Chicago, Milwaukee and other cities—to combine the Republican and Democratic electorate upon a non-partisan ticket.

Impetus will be given to the exercise of Federal power in accomplishing great social reforms if the agencies seeking these reforms do not bear the Socialist label. The leaders of the Progressive party undoubtedly had this idea in mind when they framed in 1912 a political platform which closely paralleled the utterances of the Socialist organization. It included the prevention of industrial accidents, occupational diseases, overwork, involuntary unemployment, and other injurious effects incident to modern industry; the fixing of minimum safety and health standards for the various occupations and the exercise of the public authority to maintain such standards; the prohibition of child labor; a minimum wage in all industrial occupations; the general prohibition of all-night work for women and the establishment of an eight-hour day for women and young persons; the protection of home life against sickness, irregular employment and old age by a system of social insurance; the establishment of a strong Federal commission to maintain permanent active supervision over industrial corporations; the protection of the public against fraudulent stock issues; and fully a score of other activities of the same character. The political platform of the Socialist party did not go further in the matter of industrial legislation, and advanced beyond the Progressive declaration only in the advocacy of collective ownership of public utilities and of all privately-owned commercial enterprises. As for the collective ownership idea, it is a fact that there are many men in public life to-day, in all of the political parties, who believe that the Federal government will eventually own and control all of the railroads in the United States. Unquestionably this matter will become a political issue to be decided at the polls.

Very altruistic appear some of the national reforms desired by a large mass of the people but altruism is the most effective basis of the appeal for unlimited extension of the Federal power. It inspires almost every amendment to the Constitution now pending before Congress or which has been introduced during the last ten years. It is also significant that no amendment has proposed the enlargement of State powers. On the contrary each aims to invest the Federal government with larger jurisdiction. It is the Federal power which is to be invoked to suppress the liquor traffic or regulate marriage and divorce or establish uniform hours of labor. The effort to secure a constitutional amendment to legalize woman suffrage had its inspiration in the fact that if Congress would only adopt the amendment, ratification by three-fourths of the States would impose the system upon all the other States—a much less difficult method of securing the desired result than by knocking at the doors of the legislatures of the forty-eight States. Nation-wide prohibition through the adoption of an amendment to the Federal Constitution seems also assured, especially since Mr. Bryan has openly avowed his acquiescence in this procedure despite his adherence to the doctrine of State rights in the platforms upon which he ran in his various presidential campaigns. The opponents of prohibition are relying almost solely upon the plea that the regulation of the liquor traffic is solely within the rights of the States. They are leaning upon a broken reed.

The time has passed when the Democratic party, unless it desires to invite certain defeat, will return to the ideas which it enunciated in 1840 and which it so foolishly and fatally reiterated in subsequent platforms. The political battles of the future will not be fought upon the question of limiting Federal powers. Rather will we see the political parties vying with each other in suggesting how that power can be most largely exercised for the benefit of the people; and that party which not only promises but performs may be sure of a long lease of power.

Chapter XII

FEDERAL POWER IN WAR

IN time of peace the Federal power expanded steadily. With the declaration of war against Germany on April 6, 1917, it grew by leaps and bounds.

When a great national crisis is precipitated the common cause of victory necessitates prompt and decisive action and demands the subordination of corporate and individual interest. The conflict upon which we have entered concerns the nation as a whole and not the States as separate entities. The nation, therefore, must be supreme. This is a truth so self-evident that the people not only expect Federal power to be exerted to the utmost but are disappointed if such is not the case. Democracy is not, and cannot be, efficient if all its agencies are not coördinated and directed by responsible authority. This has been demonstrated by experience; and its exposition has gone so far that the war may bring about a change in our institutions as definite as the new international boundaries which will mark the conclusion of peace. In other words, it is not impossible that the trend which has been noted as constantly developing through the centuries will find us compelled to accept the practically universal application of Federal power instead of merely recording isolated instances as in the past.

In analyzing the reasons for the situation in which the nation now finds itself, we discover three factors of compelling importance. The first, of course, is the necessity of focusing authority upon the smallest possible point. Divided responsibility is irresponsibility. Realization of this fact is fully recognized and Congress has imposed upon the President a degree of authority which makes him literally the most powerful ruler in the world. The President has not sought to evade this responsibility. On the other hand, it seems to completely accord with his own view. War was not declared until he saw fit to recommend it; and the momentous step having been taken, he has proceeded under the theory that his leadership is supreme. When Congress has hesitated to adopt his policies he has appeared before it in person to add the force of his presence to the expression of his desire; while at other times he has summoned Congressional leaders to the White House for the sole purpose of emphasizing his point of view. These occurrences have excited little protest or criticism. Every one has felt that in a period of crisis the reins of government must not be loosely held. Only by the largest exercise of Federal power could results be obtained and the jurisdiction of the President, as the embodiment of that power, has proportionately enlarged.

The second factor is the abnormal economic condition resulting from the war. Production in Europe has been necessarily curtailed through the mobilization of millions of men in the various countries and those nations which possessed facilities for safeguarding the transportation of foodstuffs and munitions of war across the seas became eager purchasers of American supplies. The very exigency of the situation compelled them to procure at any cost those things which were essential to their individual and national existence and a rise in prices was the natural consequence. This led, in turn, to a popular protest which could not pass unheeded. At the same time, our Allies could not be deprived of the assistance which they so sorely needed. Here was a problem beyond State solution. It could only be successfully met by Congress investing the President with authority to appoint Federal agents who would be clothed with the utmost degree of Federal power to discipline the profiteers, turn waste into saving, prevent hoarding for speculative purposes and to protect the people from any and all kinds of imposition. Out of this necessity was born the act, approved August 10, 1917, which provides "for the national security and defense by encouraging the production, conserving the supply, and controlling the distribution of food products and fuel." In the primitive past we relied upon the law of supply and demand, the only law with which our forefathers were acquainted; but now we attempt by the exercise of Federal power "to assure an adequate supply and equitable distribution, and to facilitate the movement of foods, feeds, fuel, including fuel oil and natural gas, and fertilizer and fertilizer ingredients, tools, utensils, implements, machinery, and equipment required for the actual production of food, feeds and fuel." The law goes even further, for it proposes "to prevent, locally or generally, scarcity, monopolization, hoarding, injurious speculation, manipulations, and private controls, affecting such supply, distribution and movement."

The word "dictator" would seem to have no place in a republic and yet the word is already accepted as a part of our national vocabulary. We have seen the agents of the Federal Food Administration Bureau entering storage warehouses owned by individuals or corporations and seizing hoarded food, converting private into public property, fixing the maximum price at which manufacturers and dealers in foodstuffs can sell their goods, and even specifying the weight of loaves of bread. We find the strong arm of the Government uplifted against any person who restricts the manufacture, supply or distribution of necessaries, or hoards them, or exacts excessive prices. Under the law all persons or corporations, other than those whose business is less than $100,000 per annum, may be compelled to operate under a Federal license issued by the President, and heavy penalties are provided for violation of the provisions of the act. The President is even authorized to purchase, store, "and sell for cash at reasonable prices," wheat, flour, meal, beans and potatoes; and thus we have reached a point where the President is by force of law converted into a wholesale produce dealer—all for the good of the people. Furthermore, "he is authorized to requisition and take over, for use or operation by the government, any factory, packing house, oil pipe line, mine or other plant, or any part thereof, in or through which any necessaries are or may be manufactured, produced, prepared or mined, and to operate the same." In fact, as the provisions of this remarkable law are read and re-read, it is difficult to imagine any avenue for the exercise of Federal power which has been overlooked.

The authority of the Fuel Administrator is on an equal plane with that of the Food Administrator. As the latter has fixed the price at which the farmer shall sell his wheat, so the former has fixed the price of coal at the mine and has compelled the maximum production, so that there can be no false inflation of prices. The law gives him full authority so to do; and further, if any producer of coal and coke fails, in the opinion of the President, to conform to the governmental prices or regulations, "or to conduct his business efficiently under the regulations and control of the President aforesaid, or conducts it in a manner prejudicial to the public interest," the President is empowered to requisition and operate the plant, not, however, without allowing just compensation.

Under the drastic provisions of this law coal dealers in the United States must coöperate with the Federal Fuel Administration or go out of business. This policy was laid down in an ultimatum sent to a Pennsylvanian firm on the 8th of December, 1917, in which the firm was advised that if refusal to coöperate continued, "the Administration will take steps to have all coal shipped to you diverted to local dealers." "It is not a time when dealers can run their own business as they see fit," was the brusque and significant message of the Fuel Administrator, and the firm was given four hours to accept the dictation of the Federal agent or close its doors. Of course, it chose the former alternative; and submission by all other coal dealers will naturally follow. It is not for them to question whether a college president, suddenly placed in the position of Federal Fuel Administrator, ought to be regarded as the last word in dictating to men who have been in the coal business all their lives. It is not for them to reason why; they are compelled to literally do or die. The representatives of the people gave power to the President; the President, in turn, delegated the administration of that power to a person of his own selection; and that person, administering the law, is supreme. The question is, of course, What will be the effect of such absolute control of private industry upon the public mind? It is true that the operation of the statute is limited to the period of the war, but if the struggle should last two, three or five years, we will have ample time to observe the effect of the legislation. Beneficent results can have only one outcome. The law will be extended indefinitely. We can also depend with reasonable certainty upon another alternative. Granting that experience demonstrates that some of the provisions are impractical or operate unjustly, it is easy to believe, in view of the extent to which the nation had gone in time of peace, that Congress will seek to remedy these difficulties by amendment rather than abandon altogether the action which has been taken.

The third factor remains to be considered. Our entrance into the war found us without men, munitions or ships. To secure all these—even if the work occupied a year—was an enormous task and not to be accomplished without utilizing Federal power to the utmost. The men were secured through a Federal Conscription Act, under which the State militias which had existed for a hundred years disappeared in a National Army. As these State increments were not sufficiently numerous, additional men had to be secured and this was done through Federal process. Never were State boundaries so entirely obliterated as in the operation of the Selective Draft. In the Civil War, men joined the Sixteenth Illinois Regiment or the Seventy-first New York Regiment and the recognized State title clung to the organization throughout the four years of service. The regiments of the National Army are designated by number and the name of the State from which the men may come is never mentioned. In the Civil War, State flags were carried into battle and are still preserved with tender regard in museums devoted to relics of that great conflict. To-day there is but one emblem—the National flag.

Federal power was invoked to compel men to serve in the army because in no other way could the requisite military force have been obtained. The same power was necessary to secure the ships to provide transportation and to supply the loss occasioned by submarine warfare. Under an act approved September 7, 1916, the United States Shipping Board was created. This board has formed the Emergency Fleet Corporation and has gone into ship-building business as a government proposition, with a capital of $50,000,000 provided out of the Federal Treasury. The government can, if it so elects, absolutely control the ship-building of the entire nation and take over, at a price to be subsequently fixed, all ships completed or in course of construction.

The army cannot be transported from the interior camps to the seaports nor can the ships receive their cargoes of men, food and munitions unless the railroads move the trains with the least possible delay. Failure of the railroads to fully measure up to this enormous task compelled Federal intervention and unification of all the railroad systems under government control is now a fact. In the past we proceeded upon the theory that competition was wise and beneficial and all pooling arrangements were prohibited by law. This theory is now abandoned and Federal power is employed, through the absorption of the railroad systems into the governmental machine, to prevent traffic congestion and delay. The unification of the railroads is the greatest undertaking ever intrusted to Federal authority; and if it can be satisfactorily conducted, the people will accept that result as a final and convincing warrant for unlimited exercise of the Federal power.

The railroads having been brought under Federal control, it was but a short step to act in similar fashion regarding telegraph and telephone communication. A threatened strike by organized labor because at least one of the telegraph companies declined to allow their employees to become unionized, brought the matter to a crisis, although in the joint resolution for which the President sought hasty action, national security and defense were emphasized. An obedient House of Representatives placed all telegraph, telephone, marine cable and radio systems under Federal control after a debate of two hours, and while the Senate undertook for a brief period to exercise an independent spirit, the will of the President finally prevailed. The vote was not unanimous, for a minority of sixteen, contending that no adequate reason for the legislation had been presented and the constitutional freedom of the press from governmental supervision was in danger, recorded themselves in the negative. Even though the period of control is limited by the joint resolution to the duration of the war, the experiment, if it proves successful, may be indefinitely prolonged.

Under the exigency of the war we have a Federal insurance system which has $50,000,000 at its command to insure ships and has been provided with $176,000,000 with which to insure the lives of soldiers and sailors. Thus we find the government entering another field of private industry, although nobody questions the wisdom of this paternal regard. In fact, the people are accepting all the manifestations of governmental authority with an acquiescence that amounts to indifference and face other far-reaching conditions without surprise.

And what of the Constitution while these new laws were being enacted? It has not been seriously considered. Men in Congress have not hesitated to openly assert in debate that the Constitution is to be consulted only in time of peace. The doctrine of constitutionality has been forgotten and the doctrine of paramount necessity obtains with more force than ever before. When a normal period returns, we may recur to the once-revered document. In the meantime, we see little that has not been swept into the all-embracing arm of the government by war legislation. Singularly enough, only one feature of our individual and national life has been omitted. We have done little to make education a national institution. We have dealt with every phase of the material world but we have left the American mind to take care of itself. No one would advocate the adoption of the Prussian system of arbitrarily feeding citizens upon government-made doctrines. We ought, however, to see that those who are to grow into citizenhood, as well as those who are already citizens, are inculcated through knowledge with the spirit of democracy, the love of liberty, a respect for law and morals, and an understanding of international justice and ideals. We need not centralize the system of education and we can guard against any attempt of a party to perpetuate itself in power through the widespread teaching of its especial doctrines. When the war has taught us, as it will, that no army can have a higher patriotism than the people back of the army, and the man in the trench can rise no higher in the realm of fortitude and sacrifice than the height reached by the nation at home, we shall realize the necessity of applying Federal authority to the immaterial as well as the material. We already have Federal control of our bodies, our going and our coming, our food and our homes. Assistance in the development of our minds must come as the direct result of the war, because one of the most serious disclosures of the war period has been ignorance concerning our national traditions and aspirations. If the States do not realize the importance of emphasizing this phase of knowledge, the national government will be compelled to undertake the work. Federal education is no more to be feared than Federal regulation. It is certainly as essential to our national safety.

Chapter XIII

FEDERALISM AND THE FUTURE

THERE is but one conclusion from the facts, which, as concisely as possible, have thus far been presented. Whether we approve or not, it must be accepted as inevitable that the development of the Federal power, persistent from the very beginning of our national history, will not only continue unchecked but will more and more be made manifest. The river is sweeping onward to the sea. It might have been possible long ago, when the nation was in its swaddling clothes, to have changed the whole character of its future existence, if the people had so determined. It is now too late, for the nation has passed out of its formative period into the full stature of manhood. The truth is, however, that the American people, as a whole, have never believed that the individuality of the States must be recognized as an essential factor in our national growth. This is demonstrated by the fact that in every contest between the so-called rights of the States and the exercise of Federal power, the latter principle has prevailed. To-day there is no longer any conflict. The tide is running all one way. It is impossible to overcome its tremendous force. The nation is being swept forward upon a tide of Federalism and the anxious fears occasionally uttered by a steadily decreasing minority are deafened by the roar of the torrent.

The people, as a mass, have no doubts. They view the future with the sublime optimism which is characteristic of the American temperament. They increase, rather than decrease, the duties and responsibilities of the Federal government because their faith in that government is supreme and because they realize that no national evil can be remedied and no national results achieved except by the force of centralized authority. There is no gainsaying the lesson which the nation has learned. Even before the present war the lottery evil was abolished, the devastating yellow fever conquered, the purity of our food guaranteed, powerful corporations regulated and the great railroads of the country compelled to treat every shipper, large and small, with absolute equality. All the laws which invest the Federal government with larger powers have accomplished the anticipated and desired results, and it may be set down as an axiom that the representatives of the people will not in the future hesitate at the acceptance of any proposition which, having in view the public welfare, is offered for their consideration. They have learned the short and direct way toward progress; and the momentum of years of accumulated experience is not to be overcome.

The *status quo* existing before the war began will never be entirely restored. This is all the more true because the advanced position which we have taken under the pressure of a crisis is not radical but evolutionary. We are, therefore, confronted with the fact that when the era of peace finally arrives we must face the necessity of a new adjustment of Federal and State governments—an adjustment made all the more difficult because of the new relations occasioned by the war. The situation is further complicated by the failure of the Constitution to provide a solution of the problem. The high regard which we feel for our great charter cannot blind our eyes to the knowledge that it fails to distinctly affirm the duties and responsibilities of the States. The last three sections of Article I detail plainly the things which a

State is forbidden to do; but the things which a State can do are hidden in provisions altogether too general in their character. We find the powers of Congress, on the other hand, specifically set forth; and it is but natural to regret that the framers of the Constitution did not have the prescience to anticipate the wisdom which marks the Act of the British Parliament of 1867 which created the present union of Canada and wherein the lines of demarcation between the Dominion, on the one hand, and the provinces, on the other, are plainly drawn. One of the sections of that act is devoted to the distribution of legislative powers, twenty-nine subjects being assigned to the Parliament, which is the Federal body, and sixteen other subjects being classified under the heading, "Exclusive powers of the provincial legislatures." The consequence is that in Canada there is comparatively little dispute as to Dominion or provincial jurisdiction because the channel of its government, unlike ours, has been plainly charted.

Beneficent as the exercise of Federal power has been, and with the certainty that it will be increased rather than diminished, we must, nevertheless, admit that unless we deal with it along new lines it is fraught with evil. Present conditions point toward an oligarchy, wherein a few men will have supreme power, and the transition from an oligarchy to an autocracy is all too brief. The problem is to preserve our democracy even under a centralized, Federalistic government. The first step toward this result is to curtail executive power. The President should be deprived of the right to veto legislation, or if that right be still continued, the enactment of a law despite his veto should be made possible by a majority vote of the two Houses of Congress. It is true that this would necessitate an amendment to the Constitution, but this is not an insurmountable obstacle. On the contrary, the time has come when constitutional changes should be boldly and persistently advocated. We are too apt to regard the Constitution as a document beyond criticism or revision. It is revered like the ark of the Covenant, not to be profaned by impious touch. President Lowell, of Harvard University, explains the origin of this reverence. "The generation that framed the Constitution," he says, "looked upon that document as very imperfect, but they clung to it tenaciously as the only defense against national dismemberment, and in order to make it popular, they praised it beyond their own belief in its merits. This effort to force themselves to admire the Constitution was marvelously successful, and resulted, in the next generation, in a worship of the Constitution of which its framers never dreamed."

It must be remembered, also, that the men who dominated the making of the Constitution were by no means convinced that the common people could be trusted. Suffrage, in the early days of the republic, even when exercised in the election of representatives of the people, was not universal, being restricted by property and other qualifications. Any action taken by the popular branch of Congress was subject to review by a Senate whose members were deliberately and carefully chosen by State legislatures; the Senate being the saucer, according to a remark attributed to George Washington, into which the hot tea of the House could be poured to cool. Should both the Senate and the House be too responsive to popular demand, there was still a refuge for property and other conservative interests in the veto power of the President and in the knowledge that it would require a two-thirds vote in both Houses to overcome his objection. The men who to-day still entertain a lurking fear of the people will undoubtedly uphold this veto power as one of the most important and necessary safeguards of the Constitution, just as they opposed the popular election of Senators. None the less, the United States stands alone to-day among the great constitutional governments in conferring upon its ruler the right to thwart the expressed will of the national legislature. In France the President has no veto power. In Great Britain, the action of Parliament is final; and in Italy, the sanction of the King "is necessary to the validity of laws proposed by the Parliament, but in point of fact he never refuses it." We have already shown the menace to our free institutions through the dispensation of patronage by the President. The privilege of wholesale appointment and the right to veto legislation must be taken away from him before we can view with entire equanimity our further certain progress along the path of Federal power.

Something is radically wrong with our system of government when the representatives of the people, charged by their oaths to perform the legislative duties for which they were duly elected, are deterred from the consideration of measures by the knowledge that even should such measures be enacted, they would be vetoed by a hostile President. When Congress is evenly divided on party lines, and when support of a President is made a solemn party obligation, the national legislature is powerless to act. Occasionally, when administration or political policies are not involved, a veto is without effect; but the fact remains that there is absolutely no reason why the judgment of a single man, even though he be the occupant of the White House, should neutralize the will of the majority of the representatives of the people in Congress.

Other steps, even more progressive, must be taken. The trouble is that while we have in practice, if not in theory, changed our whole system of government, we have not formally recognized the fact that the change has taken place. We have drifted along, in characteristic American fashion, without having the courage to confess that the old idea of State sovereignty has been wiped out of existence by the necessities of modern times. With marked persistency we are building up a centralized Federal government, reducing the States to mere nonentities, but we are making no provision for working out our salvation under the new régime. We must be blind not to see that the era of Federal power is permanently established and yet no one has had the courage to provide for the inevitable future by devising a system of government designed to meet new conditions. We are allowing the foundations of our national edifice to crumble away without planning a safe and durable substitute. If the States in our union are to drop to the plane of counties in England, or departments in France, or provinces in Canada—and already they are in this category—and we are still to preserve the democratization which has been our strength and our glory in the past, we must see to it that neither an oligarchy nor an autocracy takes the place of a republic. There is only one way in which we can avoid the peril that threatens. The government must not be centered in a president, to which point we have arrived, but must be directly administered by the people. In other words, the solution of our national problem lies in the adoption of a system of parliamentary control, similar to that which gives to Great Britain, France and Canada a centralized or national government without the evils which even now are part of our experience.

We have a traditional love for the States. They existed as independent political organizations before the republic was formed. They are now a part of our great union; and, with a love that is more sentimental than wise, we hesitate to relegate them to the position of mere provinces. Nevertheless, we must realize that the States, even if they are not all laggards in the march of progress, are prevented from unanimity of action by reason of their diversity of location and multiplicity of numbers; and disjointed action is worse than futile. The greater must swallow up the less; and the Federal ægis is over all. In readjusting ourselves to this new condition we need not do violence to the eternal principles which inspired our Constitution. We can—and, indeed, we must—eliminate certain details which are neither sacred nor lasting, and introduce those essentials which will insure the national development and permanency which other democracies enjoy. We could advantageously borrow from France the provision which gives the President a term of seven years, with ineligibility for reëlection. The parliamentary government of Great Britain is responsive and responsible; but, especially, we find in Canada a model of federal union which is worthy of serious consideration.

Students of the Canadian system insist that it contains elements of undoubted strength not enjoyed by the people of the United States. This is unquestionably true. The head of the Dominion Government is the Governor-General, appointed by the crown, but his principal duty consists in safeguarding the integrity of the empire. He governs entirely through a ministry which comes from and is responsible to the people. A weak cabinet in Canada could not long continue in power. The instinct of political self-preservation compels the selection of strong, capable men, skilled in the knowledge of the great departments which they are called upon to administer. Otherwise they cannot survive. In the United States, a presidential cabinet can be chosen for personal reasons from among the butchers and bakers and candlestick-makers, and if an obedient Senate confirms the nominations, the people have no recourse. The members of a presidential cabinet are not responsible to the people, they cannot be interrogated upon the floor of Congress, and can remain in office as long as they are *persona grata* to the President; and the weakness and inefficiency of some presidential cabinets has been little short of a national scandal. In Canada, as in England, a ministry stands or falls upon the adoption or defeat of measures which it proposes; and should defeat come, there is provision for a prompt appeal to the people upon the question at issue. We lack this elasticity in the United States. Here we elect a Senator for six years, a Representative for two years and a President for four years, during which terms nothing done by either, short of an impeachable offense, can affect his official status; and the fact that a President is to remain in office long enough to influence by praise or criticism the political fortunes of candidates in his own party seeking reëlection compels subordination to his will. This fact menaces free government. The remedy lies in recasting our system so that the President shall be surrounded by men whose period of power must end when, in the judgment of the representatives of the people, their unfitness is demonstrated by their acts.

The American people are, as a whole, so loth to interfere with established custom that even the mere suggestion of a departure from the beaten path is certain to antagonize those timid souls who are not yet willing to recognize that times have changed and that we must change with them. Nevertheless, with the fact staring us in the face that unchecked progress along the path of Federal power is as certain for the future as it has been in the past, we must provide some method which will insure the perpetuity of the republic under new conditions. We can obliterate State lines and still remain a democracy; but our principles and ideals, which are of more concern than State governments, are doomed if the strong centralized authority which we have created is allowed to operate without recognized principles and without restraint. Already, in our typically American desire to achieve immediate and decisive results, we have endowed individuals with unlimited power—a fact which gives aid and comfort to those who assert that only in this way can democracy escape failure. The great body of our citizenship are not, however, of little faith. They are sincerely imbued with the hope and belief that we can be a nation without becoming an autocracy; that Federal power can continue to be exercised without danger; and that our democracy can be preserved without minimizing efficiency or destroying the great structure of liberty which has been erected.

In presenting a plan whereby this aspiration can be realized, we do not have to resort to radical procedure. It is not necessary to hastily adopt the English form. We can approach an ideal system through gradual stages, without disrupting our Constitution, but, on the other hand, more strongly emphasizing the principles of popular government. We need not, for instance, entirely deprive the President of the appointing power. Judges and higher officials may still be selected by him, subject to confirmation by the Senate; but the great bulk of the office-holders, who deal, as it were, with the purely business side of governmental affairs, should be chosen through non-political, competitive methods and retained as long as they faithfully and effiicently perform their duties. It is true that this would play havoc with the politicians who believe that to the victors belong the spoils, but the large majority of the people who are more concerned with good administration than with the distribution of patronage, would view this new era with profound satisfaction.

The members of the cabinet who are, and always have been, personal appendages of the President, should still be appointed by him, but they should be directly responsible for their acts and policies to the representatives of the people in the Senate and House. They should have seats upon the floors of both Houses for the purpose of answering inquiries; and with each one conscious of his strict accountability to Congress, the government would be brought closer to the people. In the adoption of this plan it would be necessary to merge into the several departments the numerous bureaus, commissions and boards which now enjoy an irresponsible and unrestrained existence; but such coördination would tend to efficiency and direct responsibility. Much of the evil of an independent and constantly increasing bureaucratic system would be removed.

If it be asserted that by making cabinet officers responsible to the representatives of the people instead of to the President, the latter will be in some degree shorn of power, the answer must be frankly made that such deprivation is by no means undesirable. There is no necessity, even if it were possible, to reduce the presidency of the United States to the perfunctory position which, for example, obtains with the head of the French republic; nor is it feasible at this time to establish a premiership such as forms the pivot of the English government. We can, however, avoid the abuse and misuse of Federal power by government officials, which is not a distant menace, if the men appointed by the President to administer the great departments of the government are made directly and instantly responsible to the representatives of the people. In its actual operation the plan would differ from the English system in that Congress could deal with the cabinet individually as well as collectively; the former, if the member be manifestly inadequate, incompetent, or otherwise unfitted for his high position; and the latter, if a repudiated measure be presented as the policy of the entire administration. Certain it is that if in the past some plan such as is here suggested had been in force, the history of sundry legislative and official actions would have been less open to criticism than has been the case.

Universal acceptance cannot be anticipated for any method or methods which are offered as a solution of the problems which accompany the almost unrestricted exercise of Federal Power. The subject is too vast and complicated to be clarified by a single idea. Much will be accomplished, however, if thoughtful attention of the American people can be directed to present conditions and to the necessity of studying their effect upon our national future. We know that it would be fatal to attempt to operate a modern, broad-gauge railroad train upon the ancient rails over which Stephenson carefully maneuvered his first steam engine. The analogy applies to the

United States. We must meet new conditions, wherein the States, as integral parts of a dual plan, have almost completely vanished, and their places taken by a powerful, compact machine known as the National Government. The State will, in the future, bear the same relation to the union that the county does to the State. It will be a convenient geographical division with limited and circumscribed powers. Even its last vestige of erstwhile glory—the right to cast its electoral vote for President and Vice-President—will soon be taken. The people and not the States must decide who shall be the chief executive of the nation. This will require another amendment to the Constitution, but this change, like others, is only a matter of time.

Federal power, briefly stated, is the power of the people. It is granted in the last four words of the tenth article of the Constitution—four pregnant and significant words which have been overlooked, if not entirely ignored. "The powers not delegated to the United States by this Constitution," says the article, "nor prohibited by it to the States, are reserved to the States respectively *or to the people.*" Experience has demonstrated that the States cannot think or act nationally. Forty-eight legislatures cannot act in unison; and the evils of our modern civilization or the crises which come with succeeding generations cannot be successfully combated or overcome with the weakness and lack of cohesion which are inseparable from separate political organizations. With the passing of the States, the people are coming into their own, but in order to meet their new and tremendous responsibilities they must be provided with a system of government different in its details from that under which we have been existing, half-State and half-Nation. The people have acted under the plain grant of the Constitution in investing the Federal government with unexampled power and they have thus acted because it was evident that in no other way could the development of the nation be assured; but due regard for the safety and permanence of their government demands that they shall directly exercise this power. They should abolish the absurdity of undergoing a three months' spasm in a presidential campaign and then subsiding into a state of utter helplessness for the succeeding four years. They should revise the Constitution so as to extend the presidential term to six years, with ineligibility for reëlection; should reduce to a minimum the presidential dispensation of patronage; and provide for a cabinet which would be personally and immediately responsible to them for every official act and recommendation. Congress, representing the people, would then be free to act without fear or favor; and the pivot upon which the nation turns would no longer be the White House but the Capitol. The framers of the Constitution gave first and most extended consideration to the legislative branch of our government; and if this place of honor has not been held, it is because the evolution of Federal power has abnormally developed the position of the executive. The fact that the President has loomed larger and larger in our political history has dwarfed Congress and is the basis for the prevalent criticism that, as a body, it has retrograded in initiative, independent judgment and personnel.

There is no fear of Federal power in Great Britain, France or Canada, even though they have centralized governments. There need be no menace of Federal power in this country if, as in other great democracies, the people keep the control of that power in their own hands through a cabinet responsible to their representatives in Congress and through the restriction of executive authority. We can no longer stand upon the shifting sands of opportunism, trusting in haphazard fashion that the obsolete forms of the past will in some inscrutable way be adjusted to the inevitable exigencies of the future. We must face our duty with faith and wisdom, and, above all, with courage. We must honestly recognize the fact that the States have been eliminated as national factors and that we have established a Federal government with supreme functions; but there is still before us the task of making that government so elastic, so completely under the control of the people and so free from the perils of autocracy that Federal power, instead of being a menace to our liberties, will be the cornerstone upon which our nation will permanently endure.

Printed in Dunstable, United Kingdom

91220038R00127